PRAISE FOR *27 SUMMERS*

"This inspiring, powerful, and important memoir is so timely as we continue to reckon with decades of over-incarceration and excessive punishment. Ronald Olivier makes redemption accessible to us all."

—**Bryan Stevenson**, author of *Just Mercy*

"I picked up *27 Summers*, and I just couldn't put it down. To read this story of how God moved and changed the life of a man who was serving a life sentence is just amazing—and then to use him to change other lives. As Ronald Olivier says, 'Don't tell me what God can't do!'"

—**Tony Dungy**, *New York Times* bestselling author and NFL studio analyst

"I first met Ronald Olivier in prison—an experience I thought I would never take part in. Since meeting Ronald and learning about his story, I've wanted nothing more than for the world to hear it and meet the man who inspired me. *27 Summers* will change your perspective on life, faith, and love. Ronald did that for me. His story will do the same for you. I can't wait for you to read about Ronald and learn what I learned: that change is not only possible but also probable when you encounter Jesus. Thank you, Slim, for sharing your story with the world. We need it."

—**Sam Acho**, author, speaker, and ESPN analyst

"Ronnie Slim is a living testimony to God's redemptive power. In the depths of one of America's most notorious prisons, he discovered unimaginable healing, hope, and God's purpose for his life. *27 Summers* tells the story of God's abounding love, proving that even in the darkest of circumstances, He is with us and provides a way out."

—**Len Vanden Bos**, chaplain for the Buffalo Bills

"Gritty, terrifying, yet truly uplifting!"

—**Bear Grylls**, adventurer, author, and Emmy Award–winning television presenter

"This is one of the most compelling comeback stories you will ever read. It will hold your attention on every page—and ultimately lead you to your knees in wonder, love, and praise. Hugely recommended!"

—**Matt Redman**, author and Grammy
Award-winning worship leader and songwriter

"This inviting, encouraging, and inspiring book is the read you've been waiting for! Ronald Olivier's journey of flaws and failures led to a life of faith and unusual triumph. *27 Summers* beckons you to step behind prison walls with Ronnie and experience freedom born of God's grace and mercy, proof that He never counts anyone out."

—**Dr. Leslie Draper III**, board certified senior clinical
chaplain and mayor of Simmesport, Louisiana

"*27 Summers* is an incredible journey into the power of redemption. Ronald Olivier's story takes us on a rollercoaster from his wild youth in the streets of New Orleans to the Louisiana State Penitentiary, where he finds salvation and solace through faith in God. This book is an inspiring tale that shows how even in our darkest moments, we can find hope, peace, and freedom if we choose to turn to God. Ronald is a great example to others that anyone seeking God and redemption can find his way out of the pits of hell—from a life of crime and prison—and into a life of helping others. *27 Summers* is a must-read."

—**Commissioner Burl Cain**,
Mississippi Department of Corrections

27 SUMMERS

27 SUMMERS

MY JOURNEY *to* FREEDOM, FORGIVENESS,

and REDEMPTION *During My*

Time in ANGOLA PRISON

RONALD OLIVIER
with CRAIG BORLASE

NELSON
BOOKS

An Imprint of Thomas Nelson

27 Summers

Copyright © 2023 by Ronald Olivier

All rights reserved. No portion of this book may be reproduced, stored in a retrieval system, or transmitted in any form or by any means—electronic, mechanical, photocopy, recording, scanning, or other—except for brief quotations in critical reviews or articles, without the prior written permission of the publisher.

God's Most Precious Treasures is used with permission from Bill Yount.

Published in Nashville, Tennessee, by Nelson Books, an imprint of Thomas Nelson. Nelson Books and Thomas Nelson are registered trademarks of HarperCollins Christian Publishing, Inc.

Published in association with the literary agency of Ann Spangler and Company.

Thomas Nelson titles may be purchased in bulk for educational, business, fundraising, or sales promotional use. For information, please email SpecialMarkets@ThomasNelson.com.

Scripture quotations are taken from the King James Version. Public domain.

Names and identifying characteristics of some individuals have been changed to preserve their privacy.

ISBN 978-1-4002-3917-7 (ePub)
ISBN 978-1-4002-3912-2 (HC)

Library of Congress Control Number: 2023018253

Printed in the United States of America
23 24 25 26 27 LBC 5 4 3 2 1

In memory of Jermonce "J-Dog" Martin.
Wondering who you could have become.

CONTENTS

PART 3: LIFE OR DEATH

PART 4: THIS WAY UP

PART 5: GOD KNOWS WHERE YOU ARE

PART 6: THE ROAD TO FREEDOM

PART 7: A NEW HOME

FOREWORD

I'll never forget the first time I entered the front gates of the notori-ous Louisiana State Penitentiary, better known as Angola. It was 2007.

As I toured Angola with my friend Warden Burl Cain, I was surprised to see the vast farmlands filled with crops growing in the fields and herds of cattle grazing. But then we visited various camps, including death row, where more than five thousand prisoners were housed. These camps were vastly different than the area I had first toured. The atmosphere was ripe with hopelessness, depression, danger, and a sense of captivity I had never experienced before.

This trip was the first of my many visits to Angola, and I learned that in recent years, a revival was happening; the gospel of Jesus Christ had spread among the inmate population, producing amazing stories of changed lives. One might think these were shallow "jailhouse conversions," as the average sentence among prisons was almost ninety years. But this was not the case. Men were finding Christ, growing in their faith, and even training biblically to serve as evangelists and spiritual leaders among the prison population. In the midst of bitter regret, I met men radiating joy and faith. Multiple congregations of believers had formed and met weekly in the various chapels spread across the prison grounds. Men with little expectation of ever stepping outside Angola engaged in regular, heartfelt worship and serious Bible study. What a powerful demonstration that Jesus Christ is alive, and His grace changes situations that others call hopeless.

Before each visit to Angola, I asked if I could have lunch with six to eight believers whose testimonies had been part of the video our church produced in 2008 called *Miracle of Hope*. One of the guys present at those lunches was Ronald Olivier, who had entered Angola as a teenager. Imagine that scenario! A kid locked up and surrounded by thousands of inmates in one of the most infamous maximum security prisons in America.

Ronald had grown up in such a violent neighborhood and thought it unlikely that he would still be alive at age thirty-three. Most of his childhood friends were dead and he had assumed he would meet the same fate. In Angola Ronald experienced the power and forgiveness of Jesus and was transformed. But a life sentence was still hanging over him. In *Miracle of Hope* Ronald declared boldly that he believed God had something planned for him beyond Angola. And he held on to that belief for years.

When Ronald was released from prison, I immediately made plans for him to visit New York City and the Brooklyn Tabernacle where I pastor. I wanted the congregation to hear firsthand the testimony of God's miraculous grace in his life.

The day before he spoke, I sat alone with him at a table in a downtown Brooklyn restaurant. There we were—no longer eating prison food in a Louisiana prison with correction officers watching us, but now just two Christian friends enjoying fellowship. At one point Ronald looked at me and said quietly, "Pastor, can you believe we're really here together? Don't tell me what God can't do!"

In *27 Summers* you will read the poignant, true story of my friend Ronald Olivier.

Don't tell *me* what God can't do.

Jim Cymbala
Senior Pastor, The Brooklyn Tabernacle

PROLOGUE

27 Summers

"Twenty-seven summers."

It's dark in the cell, like it always is, but I can see the inmate clearly. He's scowling. Eyes narrowed. Fists bunched up between the bars. So I say it again, but slower this time.

"Twenty-seven summers."

There's not much background noise in this corner of the prison, and I know I've said it loud enough for the guy to hear me. But he clearly has no idea what my words mean. And I'm okay with that. It's exactly why I said it.

Let me tell you a little something about prison. If you're going to have any chance at all of surviving, you have to know how to communicate. Some of it is spoken, such as knowing that some—but not all—inmates measure time served in summers, not years. But a lot of the time it's the nonverbal communication you really must pay attention to. That man staring at you from across the TV room? Break eye contact at your peril. The inmate who offered you a cigarette on the first day you arrived in the unit? Man, you don't even want to know what he's got in mind for you.

I learned all this years ago, but the knowledge never goes away. It's like breathing. You never forget what you've got to do to stay alive.

So, whenever I'm making my rounds as chaplain, I'm careful about everything I do and everything I say. If someone turns his back on me when he sees me coming, I say hello but keep on walking, letting him know I respect his space. If someone's leaning on his bars wanting to talk, I stop and show him I'm ready to listen.

But this guy right here, the one scowling as he stands opposite me inside his cell, he needs something different. He's been shouting and cussing ever since I reached him, yelling about how there are rats in his cell and his toilet broke two weeks ago and it still isn't fixed and how he's been here for fifteen years and the conditions in Unit 29 are the worst he's ever encountered and how he's never going to get out and how someone like me could never understand because I get to go home every night while he's locked in here with the rats and the broken toilet.

He only stops talking when he pauses for a breath, and I say three words. They land on him like a spell. Like most spells, the effect is only temporary.

The inmate takes a deep breath and starts up again.

"What you talking about, man? Twenty-seven summers? What that mean? You trippin'. God can't help me in here anyway."

I move a little closer. He's staring right at me, his eyes locked on mine. If we were both inmates and there weren't bars between us, he'd be getting ready to strike. But I'm not going to break the stare. I need him to know I'm serious. I want him to listen to every word I'm about to say.

"You've been here fifteen?" I say. "Well, I did twenty-seven summers in Louisiana State Penitentiary. Angola. I had life without benefit of parole or probation. I was supposed to die in prison. I was locked up twelve years longer than you've been locked up, and now I'm standing here. I'm the director of chaplaincy right here at Mississippi State Penitentiary. I'm in front of your cell, talking with you today, and I'm free.

"There seemed to be absolutely no light at the end of the tunnel for me, but there *was* a light in the tunnel. I embraced that light, and the light embraced me, and it led me to the end of the tunnel. That light is Jesus Christ, so don't tell me what God can't do!"

The inmate doesn't say anything. He doesn't stop staring either. But now his eyes aren't challenging me. He's not looking for a fight. He's looking for hope.

And maybe he's just found some.

PART I

THE STREETS

1 | THE PARTY

My story begins the day I became like most of the other kids I knew living in the Eighth Ward of New Orleans: fatherless. It was the day my dad moved out of Louisiana. The day I never imagined would happen. The day I was unprepared for. The day the planets spun out of control.

Dad hadn't shared a house with us for years, but he'd never lived more than a few blocks away. Wherever he was living he'd always come get us so we could spend time with him. His first wife, Momma Brenda, had given him three kids: Reggie, Janeé, and Tiny. My parents were never married, and my mama had another child, Penny, from another relationship—but it didn't stop Dad from treating her as if she were his very own. He'd scoop all of us kids into the car on weekends, and we'd spend long summers together, just one big family.

So even though he remarried and had a kid, April, with his second wife—a force of nature we called Lil Mama—I saw my dad all the time when I was growing up. He took us fishing, took us on cruises, and took us to Mardi Gras. He was a constant in my life, always guiding me, always influencing me, always reminding me of the right thing to do and the right way to do it. I was pretty strong-willed as a kid, but like the moon controls the ocean tides, my dad kept me on the right path. He used his belt when he had to, but the conversation that followed was always more important than the whippin'.

"What did you do wrong?" he'd say when he was done with the belt. "And what are you going to do different next time?"

But while he was strong enough to control me, my dad wasn't able to hold back the bank. A few runs of bad luck turned into a financial disaster, and pretty soon the bank foreclosed on his house. With no hope of getting a job in New Orleans, my dad and Lil Mama relocated to Jacksonville, Florida, in pursuit of a fresh start.

Everybody loved my dad and Lil Mama, so the farewell party was epic. Q93, NOLA's best hip-hop and R&B station, brought the sound system and the drinks and broadcast much of the party. My dad grilled a table's worth of steaks and ribs, and Lil Mama spent all morning frying chicken and making party sandwiches.

Even though their house was packed into boxes, I was in denial. I blocked out the conversations I was overhearing—which all seemed to be about how much people were going to miss Dad, Lil Mama, and April, or what life would hold for them in Florida. Instead, I concentrated on what mattered most to me as a fifteen-year-old boy: the music, the alcohol, and the girls.

The music was good. When the DJ wasn't trying to please Dad by playing Earth, Wind & Fire, he laid down a little New Orleans bounce music and the Geto Boys. A couple of times, we even got a little N.W.A.

I was doing okay with alcohol at the party too. These were the days of wine coolers, and I discovered a deep love for peach-flavored Cisco. It made my vision go a little blurry after a while, but I found that as long as I kept on eating Lil Mama's fried chicken, it seemed to soak up the alcohol.

And girls? Well, let's just say my flirting game was pretty good for a fifteen-year-old kid.

At some point my brother Tiny and I found ourselves in an empty room with just a bed in it. We were lying there, staring at the ceiling. The reality that Dad was leaving sank in. And fast. Soon we were both crying. Mama came in at some point, and she tried to comfort us. It was no use.

When Dad came in, he climbed on the bed, got right in there between us. He held us tight.

"I'm not leaving y'all like a pack of dogs. I will send for y'all. Bring you to Jacksonville to live with me and Lil Mama. You like that?"

We lay on the bed for the longest time. Dad holding us all in close, stronger than the fullest of moons. I remember wanting to stay there forever but knew it wouldn't last. Sooner or later, he would stand up. Sooner or later, he would leave.

I don't remember much of what was said after that, but I know exactly what I was thinking: I was convinced I was never gonna see him again. After all, almost nobody I knew in the Eighth Ward ever saw their dad. Some people I knew had said goodbye to theirs—at hospital bedsides, on the other side of prison bars, or maybe even at farewell parties like this one—but most of them had never even known their fathers in the first place. In the Eighth Ward, dads were like an exotic species that was just about to become extinct.

So finally, with mine about to leave for what I believed would be forever, I was just like every other fifteen-year-old kid I knew.

And that meant one thing.

It was about time I became a man.

2 | RUNNING THE STREETS

"**Ronnie Slim!** *Ronnie Slim!* **Someone's looking out the window of the** house. Let's ghost."

I could hear Leekie loud enough, but I wasn't listening. I was blocking him out just like I was blocking out the flashing lights and blaring horn of the car alarm.

"Let me try that!"

That was J-Dog, the other member of our little trio. I wasn't listening to him either. I was busy trying to break the steering collar on an Oldsmobile Ninety-Eight.

Back in the 1990s, you only really needed two things to steal a car. The vehicles were simpler and a lot less secure than they are today, so the only tool required to get inside was a regular flathead screwdriver. Then you'd break the collar of the tilt steering wheel and pull the pin on the side to start the car. After that you just had to go through the blinker box to release the steering wheel.

But the second thing you needed wasn't something you could pick up at a hardware store or figure out by playing around with an abandoned car on the side of the road. You needed speed. Without it, you'd probably end up dead.

A lot of the cars in the neighborhood had alarms back then. Where we lived, people depended on their cars and were kind of protective of them. Owners had a habit of reacting quickly whenever their vehicles started wailing and the lights started flashing. So, most of the time, you didn't have long before the owner would hear the alarm, run to the window, and start shooting at you.

How long, exactly, was hard to say. But we figured it was about ten seconds.

Leekie, J-Dog, and I had done our research. We had started stealing cars shortly after my dad left, spending a few weeks figuring out how to do it right and which one of us did it best. We discovered I had a real talent for auto theft, and so far, I hadn't encountered a steering collar I couldn't break.

That is, until this particular night and this particular car. It was my first time trying to get into a Ninety-Eight, and my trusty screwdriver was too small for the collar. I could jam it in good enough, but the collar simply wouldn't break. The more I tried, the sweatier my hands became.

"That's twelve sec—"

Leekie's voice was drowned out by the sound of a bullet hitting a trash can behind us.

The next shot followed almost immediately—this time even closer to the target—but before the third bullet came in, I finally was able to break the collar. Pulling the pin and releasing the steering wheel was a lot easier than the collar, and soon we were burning rubber and speeding away.

I wasn't just good at stealing cars either. Turned out I was a natural joyrider too. I could corner at speeds that made my friends regret not wearing their seatbelts. I could jump every red light and run every stop sign without ever having a collision. More importantly, I seemed to have some weird sense about things. I could tell when a car was going to be too closely guarded to steal or when the police were too close to escape. I never knew how I knew; I just knew.

Leekie and J-Dog had their own unique talents too. They were both older than me—Leekie by one year and J-Dog by two—and Leekie was definitely the wisest one with the coolest head. He would always pause whenever we thought we'd found a good car to steal. Then he'd take a few moments to look around and tell us if he thought we'd be particularly vulnerable to a shooter, which was exactly what he'd said as soon as we'd seen the Ninety-Eight.

J-Dog was a hothead. He was explosive and took more risks than any of us. Unlike Leekie and I, who'd spent all our lives on the same street in the Eighth Ward, J-Dog had spent most of his life living in the Desire Projects. The neighborhood isn't there anymore, but to anyone living in New Orleans in the '80s and '90s, the Desire Projects were infamous and terrifying. It was a jungle in there. Lawless and violent. Kill or be killed. Only the lions survived.

If Leekie was wise and J-Dog was wild, I was right in the middle. Some days I could see Leekie's point of view and would be persuaded to back down from something stupid. Most of the time I found myself going along with whatever crazy idea J-Dog suggested, which meant Leekie was outnumbered and would always choose to come along with us.

The streets were our playground, and we did whatever we wanted. We could steal cars, race them all over the neighborhood, and leave them broken and bleeding in the middle of the road. Nobody could stop us. There were never any consequences. It was better than any video game you could ever imagine. Pretty soon I was so addicted to the feeling of being jacked with adrenaline that I wanted to get my fix every night.

Maybe it was because we'd nearly been shot by the owner of the Ninety-Eight, but the adrenaline was particularly strong that night. I peeled out of the Seventh Ward on St. Bernard Avenue pushing eighty miles an hour. I caught air as we crossed North Claiborne and slammed a hard left onto North Robertson. The police sirens struck up right away.

"Ronnie Slim!" Leekie yelled, but there was nothing to say. As long as I was driving, Leekie and J-Dog were in my hands. I was going to do whatever I was going to do.

It must have been three or four in the morning, and the streets were practically deserted. I took the shortest route possible back to the Eighth Ward and trusted that I knew the backstreets better than the police did. I had the added advantage of not knowing what the Ninety-Eight's limits were. I took every corner as fast as possible and kept the engine in the red the whole time.

Eventually I slowed right down, aiming for a good place to abandon the car—somewhere close enough to home that we'd only have to jump a few fences. The sirens had faded, but it was only a matter of time before they would find us again.

We crawled for a few minutes until we made a right turn and came face-to-face with a patrol car. He was a hundred feet ahead. He hit the gas. I spun left. Toward a dead end.

The engine was screaming. We were only a few blocks from mine and Leekie's street, and the roads were narrow and empty. The road ended in a wooden fence three or four hundred feet up ahead, and we were pushing sixty.

"Ready?"

Neither of them spoke. They knew what was coming—an audacious move that would help us vanish like magicians. If it worked. We'd tried it the last time we'd stolen a car, but it hadn't worked then. I figured I just hadn't been going fast enough.

I pushed the engine. There was only a little road left. The siren was closer now, and the blue lights shone through the back window.

I didn't pay the police car any attention. All I focused on was the end of the road up ahead.

One hundred feet.

Fifty.

Forty.

"Now!" I yelled. I kept my foot on the gas and slammed the gearshift into Park. Our speed tanked, and all hell broke loose in the engine bay. The car started flailing like a corpse plugged into a power line. There was a smell of burned oil, heat, and metal and—just as I'd hoped—a quickly forming cloud of thick, white smoke billowing out from under the hood.

Within a couple of seconds, we had ourselves the perfect cover for our escape. The police couldn't see us through the smoke, and we ran away undetected.

Four minutes, seven fences, and three blocks later, I was back home.

I lay in bed, my heart still sprinting. There was no way I would be able to sleep, but that didn't matter. I was happy just to lie there and replay the events of the evening. It had been a good one. Earlier we'd been down on Canal Street eating chicken at Popeyes. J-Dog had robbed a guy of his Starter jacket. Leekie had gotten a girl's number. And then I'd got us in the car.

A perfect way to celebrate my sixteenth birthday.

3 | FLORIDA

If my dad is like the moon—strong and steady and holding us near with his love—then my mom is like the sun. She's also loving, and a whole lot of her gravitational pull keeps her family close. But unlike my dad, she runs hot. She burns bright. She's a chemical reaction waiting to explode. Her whole family's like that, and I couldn't count how many family barbecues I've attended that ended with some of them brawling down there on the street and the police getting called.

But I have never doubted her love for me. Even when I was running wild and stealing cars, I knew it then.

I knew it from the hugs and kisses she gave me.

I knew it from the seventy-hour weeks she put in at her two jobs.

I knew it from the way she and Leekie's mom would be standing on the porch at four or five in the morning, waiting for us to return. We'd walk back—or run if the police were involved—and they'd both start screaming and yelling at us. It was loud, and sometimes a little violent. But it was love. The pure, fierce, sun-burning love of a mama for her children.

But even though I never once doubted her love for me in those days—and never have since—I also knew she could not control me. I was her son, and that meant I blazed just as fierce and bright as she did. With no father around to keep me in check, I was uncontrollable.

After eight months of running wild with Leekie and J-Dog, stealing cars, robbing, drinking, and being chased home by the police, something had to change. It was time to leave.

I don't remember whether it was my dad's suggestion, an order from my exhausted mom, or just a desire I'd held in my heart since the day of the farewell party. In truth, it was probably a little of everything. And I was okay with the idea of leaving New Orleans. As much as I enjoyed the thrill of stealing cars and doing whatever I wanted, I liked the idea of living somewhere different. Somewhere quieter. Somewhere that felt more like home.

I arrived in Jacksonville, Florida, at the start of the long summer vacation. I was happy, thinking my move to live with my dad would be permanent. He had finally got himself situated in a house a little ways out of the city. It was an old place with a lot of space around it, not far from a graveyard. If there were neighbors, they were too far away for us to really notice.

One of the first things that hit me was the smell.

"It's well water," said Dad as he showed me the source, ten or more open bottles that he and Lil Mama had set out all over the kitchen. "We don't get no mains water here, so we get it from the well. We set the water out like this for a couple of days, and it tastes a little better. Don't do nothing about the smell though. But you gets used to it after a while."

He was right, and within a few days I only really noticed the smell when I took a shower. What I could not get used to, however, was the silence. No traffic, no sirens, no people shouting outside our door, no gunshots, no car chases, no drug addicts, no pimps, no dealers cruising the hood with their music shaking the walls of our house.

There was just silence.

Today I'd call it peace or tranquility, but back then it felt like torture. It was like the silence you hear when you're a little kid and you wake up from a nightmare. You listen for the familiar background sounds that comfort you and tell you everything's okay and normal. When you don't hear them, the fear inside only grows.

In Florida I couldn't handle the peace. It disturbed me all the way down to my core, and I didn't have any way of understanding why at the time. Even if I could have handled the silence, I'd never have admitted that those eight months of running wild in New Orleans had already shaped me. I'd learned that when you're out on the street, you can't ever completely switch off or relax. Danger is everywhere, and you have to be ready to defend yourself at any moment.

There was one more problem. My dad. Specifically, his rules. For the first time in my life, I had a curfew.

"Midnight?" I said when he first told me what time he expected me home.

"That's right."

"Man, you trippin'."

Dad just shrugged. I took a step back, spreading my arms wide in my 49ers Starter jacket, trying to make myself look like I was a force to be reckoned with. I was five feet ten and barely a hundred pounds.

Dad just smiled. "Midnight, Ronald."

———

Being five hundred miles away didn't stop me from spending time with Leekie, J-Dog, and other friends. It didn't stop me from getting involved in a little minor criminal activity, either, as I found a way to run up thousands of dollars' worth of phone calls without them appearing on Dad's bill. I'd just call the operator, then tell them I was away from home and needed to make a call. I'd give the operator some random number, and they'd charge whatever hours-long party line followed to some innocent bill payer.

I kept myself acquainted with everything going on at home in the Eighth Ward. I heard about shootings and murders, people getting sent to juvie, and times when Leekie and J-Dog narrowly avoided getting caught by the police. They told me about getting drunk on 8-Ball and peach-flavored Cisco. They spun stories of them walking down Bourbon Street and seeing how many girls' numbers they could get. They talked about gumbo, boiled crawfish and crabs, Popeyes chicken, and foot-long po'boys with hot sausage, lettuce, tomato, and a fried egg right there on top. I could almost taste home whenever we talked.

Before the summer was over, I was back.

4 | THE FOUR HORSEMEN

Returning home meant going back to school. I'd failed ninth grade at Pierre A. Capdau Junior High and was too embarrassed to re-enroll there, so I transferred to Francis T. Nicholls High School. My attendance had never been all that great wherever I went to school, but a few significant factors helped me feel good about the start of the new school year.

First, the girls. They didn't mind me changing in their locker room. They always laughed when I'd show them whatever underwear I'd borrowed from my brother Reggie that day. (Pro tip: Leopard print wins every time.)

Another reason was math. I loved math. It completely captivated me. Whenever I was working through a page of problems, nothing else mattered. I was focused, diligent, and dedicated in that moment, battling my way to the correct answer.

The last factor that pulled me to school were my friends. J-Dog went to Charles J. Colton Junior High, but Leekie was with me at Nicholls. There were others who hung with us too—four guys called Runn, Black, Cleve, and Putt—and we were starting to get tight. We liked the fact that we had a reputation, that people on the street were starting to talk about us and give us respect. We weren't a gang exactly, but we did decide to make our organization a little more official and give ourselves a name. For some reason all the guys didn't want in, so it was just Leekie, J-Dog, Putt, and me who teamed up. Once we'd agreed on the name, the four of us took a trip to Canal Street where

we bought black FOG caps and paid to have our new name embroi-
dered along the side.

The Four Horsemen.

We were now official. We were convinced we would rule the city
one day.

––––––

But even the appeal of a locker room full of laughing girls, a perfectly
completed page of algebra, or walking down the corridor with the
Four Horsemen and knowing everybody was turning to look faded in
time. My attendance slipped, and before too long I'd stopped paying
any attention to the place. School was my past. My future was on the
streets.

Leekie and I both had older brothers. They were just like every
other eighteen- or nineteen-year-old man in the neighborhood. They
had no official job and no plans of getting one. They spent their days
sleeping or playing a little basketball, and their nights making a ton
of money selling crack.

In the absence of any other male role models, our older brothers
demonstrated what it meant to be a man. They showed us what it took
to survive and what it meant to be respected. They had the cars, the
guns, and the thick rolls of cash to prove their success. We idolized
them, plain and simple.

So it was never really a question of *if* we would start dealing
drugs, but *when*. And given that I was just sixteen and Leekie was not
yet seventeen—which, as we understood it, meant we were too young
to be prosecuted as adults for any crime we committed—there was no
good reason we could think of to wait.

The only problem was getting hold of the drugs themselves. There
were a few dealers in the Eighth Ward, but they were selling small
amounts—single rocks or an eighth of an ounce. To make a profit we

needed to buy a quarter ounce, minimum, which meant scoring from a bigger dealer. And the only place we knew anyone like that was in the Desire Projects.

Putt was more of a football player than a drug dealer, so he was out. I'm guessing Leekie was being cautious, too, because he didn't play any part in our first score either. But J-Dog and me, we were ready.

————

The Desire Projects were like most other projects back then—poor, lawless, and the kind of place everybody avoided, especially the cops. The projects spread over one hundred acres and housed more than ten thousand people, and if you absolutely, positively had to visit, you only ever went to the buildings along the front edge by the road, and you only ever visited in daylight. If you did happen to stray toward the back of the projects and didn't know the right person, you really didn't have much chance of getting out alive.

It was late and dark when J-Dog and I met at Johnny's Barroom to make sure we had the fifty dollars we needed for our purchase. I did a good job of hiding my nerves as we rode the few blocks north, and I was able to keep my voice sounding calm when we stepped onto the street that marked Desire's front boundary.

"Does he live near here?" I asked.

"No." J-Dog smiled. He knew what I meant. "In the back."

I wanted to say something to let him know I was cool with whatever, but my throat had seized up.

I followed along as J-Dog led me deep into the projects. In the bright orange streetlights, every housing block looked the same. There were no street signs or names to follow, and the only identifying features were burned-out cars. Pretty soon I was totally lost.

"We wait here," said J-Dog as we rounded a corner. He stopped under a streetlight and stared at a walkway up ahead. It was completely dark. Like staring into a cave.

"What happened to the lights?"

J-Dog shrugged. "They got shot out."

I took a look around us. It was not long after midnight, but barely anybody was out. It seemed more like Florida than New Orleans. I was going to ask J-Dog whether it was usually quiet like this when I saw a light shine in the darkness up ahead at the end of the block. It was a flashlight, pulsing on and off.

J-Dog didn't say anything. He just started walking toward the light.

I followed close behind, not letting him get more than a couple of paces ahead of me.

When we got twenty feet away from the flashlight, it stopped pulsing and shone in full. The shadows it cast were strange and hard to see at first, but eventually I could tell that ahead of us was a whole load of branches that had been pulled across the street. They formed a barrier and forced us to switch back left and right as we approached, like cattle going for slaughter. If their aim was to intimidate us, they succeeded.

There were two guys at the end of the flashlight. Both were heavily armed, and each one must have weighed at least as much as J-Dog and me combined. Nobody spoke as they made sure we had no weapons, then they sent us round a corner in the direction of another flashlight.

After a few more minutes, we were eventually shown inside an apartment. It was all pretty regular looking, with a bunch of guys my brother Reggie's age lying around, smoking, and drinking. The only difference was that Reggie and his friends kept their pistols out of sight. These guys had their assault rifles, AK-47s, and Choppers on display for everyone to see.

J-Dog handled the transaction, handing over our money and receiving half in return. I tried to look like I did this kind of thing every day.

It was only as we were leaving that I realized the most dangerous part of the deal was still ahead of us. We'd given them our money, were known to be unarmed, and now J-Dog had a half of crack in his pocket. If anyone wanted to rob us right now, it would be the easiest take ever.

We stepped out of the building, back into the darkness.

I'd never felt so powerless.

———

The next night, back in the safety of the Eighth Ward, we were ready to get to work. Leekie, J-Dog, and I had spent plenty of time talking to our brothers about how to sell, and we'd developed a solid plan for our enterprise. One of us would handle the sale, another would handle the drugs, and the third would keep watch for trouble. We'd identified our location—a street corner two blocks from our house, near a bar—where we knew nobody was dealing anywhere close.

When night fell, we assumed our positions and started selling.

Ten minutes later we had sold out. We had doubled our money in less time than it took us to walk home.

We were amazed. We knew there was easy money to be made selling crack—after all, why else would so many people we knew be doing it? But making a fifty-dollar profit in just ten minutes? Crazy.

And it was also addictive.

Before long, we took our hundred dollars back to the Desire Projects to score again.

5 | SO MUCH MONEY, SO MUCH DESPAIR

It took around two months for us to progress from dealing in half and eight balls at $50 and $125 each, to buying and selling quarters for anything from $250 to $375. All it took was a couple of hours out there on the street, and at the end of each evening, we'd each walk home with hundreds of dollars hidden away in our shoes or socks.

For the first few deals we felt like kings, but the streets have a way of reminding you who's really in charge. All it took was the low, loud rumble of a car stereo and the sight of some guy rolling into the hood, and we'd remember we were still just little fish in a very big ocean. These guys, with their teeth capped in gold and heavy chains around their necks, were the great white sharks. Their cars were monuments to their power and status, and the best of them were so impressive that the whole neighborhood would come to a halt to stand and stare. My favorite was an Oldsmobile Cutlass that belonged to a guy my brother knew. It had a green wood paint job, with gold metal flakes that caught the sun and made it look like it was made of the ocean. It had a peanut butter–colored ragtop, and the best Trues and Vogues— chrome rims and immaculate tires—that I'd ever seen.

We weren't making enough money to buy a car—and even if we were, stealing cars was still a real thrill for us. But we did at least agree that it would be cool for us to get a little gold in our mouths. Leekie had six teeth capped at $110 apiece, and J-Dog had four. I didn't like to admit it, but I was scared of needles. I had only two done, and only after I'd walked around with gold foil stuck on my teeth for a couple of weeks so my mother would think it was only paper later.

We lived in a world that was identical to what N.W.A., the Geto Boys, and all the others were rapping about. They drove the same cars we saw on the street, talked like us, dressed like us, and fought and died like us. Maybe some other version of life was taking place elsewhere in America, where people had steady jobs and quiet streets and lived to grow old and gray, but that life wasn't ever going to be mine. That version of America was about as relevant to me as life on Mars. My reality was just the way N.W.A. described it: wild, violent, and sure to be brief.

———

The most disturbing thing about dealing crack wasn't visiting our suppliers in the Desire Projects. It was dealing with our customers. We got to see how powerfully addictive crack is and how easily it can devastate a life. Addicts would steal anything they could just to get the ten dollars for a rock. When they had no money, they'd offer us anything they thought we might want. Their TV. The food in their freezer. The freezer itself. And most women offered their bodies.

The worst encounter happened early one morning, a few days before Christmas. I was bored, sitting around at home waiting for everyone else to wake up, so I took a walk around the neighborhood. I had a little crack in the pocket of my 49ers jacket just in case I saw someone who wanted to buy, but I wasn't really looking hard for a sale. It was cold outside, and I just wanted to kill time.

The streets were quiet, and I wasn't paying much attention to where I was going. But when I heard someone calling my name and banging on a window, I looked up. I saw that I had just walked by a crack house.

I stopped.

The front door was opening, and I instantly recognized the woman coming out of it. I'll call her Kim, and she was the mother of a kid I knew from school. He'd asked to join the Four Horsemen many times. He'd never been accepted.

"Ronnie Slim," Kim said. "Wait!"

She shuffled over the concrete path, arms wrapped around her in place of the belt missing from her frayed bathrobe. She was sweating, though the outside temperature must have been four below. I looked down. She was barefoot. Was she not in agony standing there like that?

"Just one rock. Please?"

"You got money?"

Her face twitched. "I got it inside."

She turned and took a step back toward the open door, then checked to see if I was following.

"I can pay," she said when she saw I hadn't moved. "I can."

I didn't like going inside crack houses, but standing still was making me feel cold. Either I was going to bounce or make the sale. I chose the sale.

Kim's house wasn't any different from the last crack house I'd been inside. There was no power, no heating, no furniture. The carpet had all been ripped up and removed—probably to pay me for a rock—and the floor was covered with newspaper, used-up lighters, and burned-up cigarettes.

Kim had disappeared into another room as soon as I got inside, and I heard her crashing around in the back. It was only when I heard a noise behind me that I realized I wasn't alone in the room. A kid was also in there. Four years old, maybe five. He was sitting on the floor, playing with an old bottle.

"I got these," Kim said as she came back into the room. She had an armful of Christmas presents that were still wrapped.

When she saw me hesitate, she pushed the presents into my arms.

"There's nothing wrong with them. They're good toys. You got a little brother?"

I looked back at the kid. His eyes were set on the presents.

"You keep them," I said. "They're his."

Kim looked anxious. "I need to score. What else do you want?" Her hands dropped, and she started to open her bathrobe. "Me?"

I told her no. She was sweating more, her breaths growing shallow and rapid.

"He's got a sister," she said, looking at the kid. "She's eight. Real pretty. You can have her. Want me to go wake her?"

My skin was crawling. I wanted to get out quickly. I would have run just then, but she was blocking the doorway.

"Listen," I said, taking the rock out of my pocket. As soon as she saw it, her eyes were locked. "You don't have ten dollars, that's fine. Pay me some other time." I held out the crack, luring her away from the door as if she were an animal I wanted to escape. As soon as she had the drugs in her hand, she pulled out a pipe from her bathrobe and started searching for a working cigarette lighter.

I left.

I'd never been so relieved to be out in minus four degrees.

6 | GUNS

The first time I ever saw someone killed, I was twelve. I woke up to the sound of shouting outside my bedroom. It was the middle of the night, but I was instantly awake. I looked out my window in time to see two men facing each other. One of them pulled out a gun and fired three shots. The other man fell to the ground as if all the muscles in his body had suddenly disappeared. The shooter paused, took a step closer to check, fired one more shot into the guy's head, then left.

The thing that really got me wasn't how sudden it all was or how close it was to my house. It was the way the shooter left. He didn't look scared and start running. He didn't even take a look around to see whether there had been any witnesses.

He just walked.

Death—or to be more specific, murder—was all around when I was running wild. Throughout Mardi Gras, New Orleans would be painted green, yellow, and purple. The rest of the time, out in the streets where the tourists never visited, the primary colors we saw were yellow and black. The colors of police tape.

Every few days I'd see evidence of another murder, and it got so that Leekie, J-Dog, and I would read the reports of the previous day's killings the way other guys read the sports news.

"Says here that your man Tariq from the Sixth got himself shot and killed."

"Where?"

"Uh . . . Lemme see . . . Seventh Ward. St. Bernard Projects."

"Alone?"

"Think so."

"Huh. Sounds right. Tariq was always leaving himself exposed."

We treated it light, but that didn't mean we didn't take it seriously. Deep down I think we were all convinced that the same fate was lying in wait for us too. It was only a matter of time before someone put a bullet in me, Leekie, or J-Dog. With so many people who looked like us dying every week, death seemed inevitable.

My reaction to all this was complex, a little hard to understand. It didn't make me scared—after all, what's the point in fearing what you're powerless to prevent? But it did rob me of peace. Every time I was out, I was hyperalert, always looking over my shoulder. I guess I was a little like someone with advanced terminal cancer: I'd accepted that I was going to die, and soon. I even embraced it, knowing that at some point I was going to be next. But I wasn't happy about it. I refused to make my peace with death until the very last moment. When I died, I'd die fighting.

———

As the 1990s began, the crack epidemic raged, and New Orleans changed. Ward by ward and street by street, the number of addicts grew. Dealers simply couldn't keep up with demand, selling what they had as soon as they'd scored. And with so many dealers walking around with thousands of dollars stashed in their shoes, they became targets.

A whole new industry developed as entrepreneurial criminals figured that instead of having to score drugs and go through the pain of dealing with crackheads, they could streamline the process and make just as much money by robbing the dealers themselves. All they needed was a gun.

Trouble was, once the robbers had been preying on dealers for a while, they got lazy and forgetful about whom they'd already stolen from. They might just be pumping gas or going about normal life in their neighborhood, when one of the dealers they'd robbed would see them and want revenge. A lot of guys got killed that way. But instead of making the decision to do their robbing farther away from where they lived, a lot of robbers took a simple course of action. They streamlined the process even more by simply killing any dealer as soon as they'd robbed them.

And so, in the space of year, it seemed as if everyone on the streets started carrying a gun. Those who didn't were almost guaranteed to die. And with all those guns around, the sound of gunfire became even more commonplace. There were times when every night sounded like the Fourth of July. It got so bad that even the birds stayed away.

———

By the time I was sixteen I had grown to five feet eleven, but at 110 pounds I was still very much on the shrimpy side. Between my physique and my naturally innocent, babyish face—and despite my two gold teeth and attitude—I suspected that I looked like easy prey out there on the street.

If I was in any doubt, I had it confirmed the night I was sitting on Leekie's porch. I felt a little uncomfortable being down on street-level like that, always preferring to be up on the raised porch outside my house, but it wasn't late and the two of us were only going to sit for a few minutes while we decided what to do that night.

Neither of us recognized the car as it approached, but we both recognized the handgun pointing right at us when the passenger window rolled down. It was a Beretta 9mm, fifteen-plus-one capacity. The driver jumped out with a .44 Bulldog, and we were very familiar with its vicious bark.

"Take off the jacket," said the guy with the Beretta as he stepped out of the passenger side of the car.

I hesitated. I'd been through a lot with my 49ers jacket, and I didn't want the trouble of finding a replacement, either legally or illegally. I also had been on the streets long enough to have trained myself not to show any fear or weakness. So I just stayed where I was. Motionless. Silent.

The guy took a step toward me, put a bullet in the chamber, and held the gun inches away from my face. "You think I'm playin'?"

I snapped out of it. Quickly the jacket was off my back and in his hands.

———

It was inevitable that I would steal myself a replacement jacket. It was also inevitable that soon after getting robbed like this, Leekie, J-Dog, and I started to carry guns regularly. All of us had been around weapons since we were little kids, and we'd borrow guns from older brothers whenever we felt like we needed them. But enough was enough. I needed to be armed 24-7.

Getting my own gun was easy. I knew a drug-addicted security guard who was desperate. For fifty dollars' worth of crack, he gave me his .38 Special, several rounds of ammunition, and a leather holster. It fit perfectly around my back, keeping the gun hidden beneath my replacement 49ers jacket but within easy reach. Wearing it as I went out to deal with my business, I felt like I was six feet two and 180.

———

The first time I fired the gun in anger, things didn't go as planned.

I'd been at Leekie's house playing Nintendo in the afternoon. The

.38 was still new to me, and I'd left the safety on in case Leekie's little brother picked it up. But Leekie, being a whole lot wiser than me, had emptied it of ammo.

I bounced later that evening with my gun in my holster, and Leekie stayed home but forgot to either put the bullets back or tell me he'd taken them out in the first place. I went to a liquor store, hoping to buy some Cisco. The clerk refused and called the security guard over. He was easily 250 pounds of prime New Orleans muscle, and he wasn't in the mood for a discussion. "Leave," he announced. It wasn't so much a request—just a statement of what he was sure was going to happen.

Usually, I'd have backed off. I'd been refused service plenty of times before. All I had to do was go outside and ask someone else to buy the wine for me. But I had my gun and my jacket, and I didn't feel much like playing by their rules.

I pulled back my jacket to reveal my gun sitting there in its holster. I told the clerk and the security guard very clearly that I was going to buy me some Cisco.

The clerk looked pale. The security guy looked mad. Neither of them showed any sign of obeying my command.

So I pulled the gun out.

Still, nobody moved.

I raised it to the security guard.

He stood perfectly still. "You don't want to do that," he announced.

He was mistaken. At that moment, in that store, he couldn't have been more wrong. I *did* want to use my gun. So I fired. Three times. Right at his chest.

Click. Click. Click.

For a fraction of a second I was confused. I'd fired the gun a few times before and knew that it worked. Why wasn't it firing now?

When the guy reached for his gun, I stopped wondering and started running.

———

The incident didn't put me off using the gun. If anything, it made me bolder. The way I saw it, if people knew I had a gun and was prepared to use it, they'd also know I was serious. Aggression was my best form of defense.

This wasn't an unusual way of thinking, and my logic wasn't controversial. Everywhere I looked I saw guys carrying guns. They'd wear a tank top tight enough to reveal the outline of the piece sticking out of the waistband of their pants. If we heard of someone shooting another guy, our opinion of them improved. If they killed someone, we didn't think badly of them. On the contrary, their actions just proved they were to be taken even more seriously.

It was the same with the victims. If someone got shot and survived, there was no shame. They didn't hide away or appear weak in our eyes. People who got shot and survived appeared stronger, as if they were invincible. "They can't kill me," you'd hear people say if they survived a shooting. They'd show their wounds and make sure everyone heard the truth: "Everything's bouncing off me. Ain't nothing can kill me."

The same was true with prison. Getting locked away was like going to college. When you came out, it was like you'd graduated. You had a new status on the street, had earned a double dose of respect. Not only had you proven to the world that you were prepared to die to defend yourself, but you had survived the dangers of prison. We might have been deluded about guns and violence, but prison was one thing we were all clear on. We knew it was dangerous behind those bars. The things that happened in there were the stuff of nightmares.

Even though I was one of the few people I knew of who still had contact with his dad, I wasn't alone. There was one other guy in the neighborhood who knew who his dad was and still saw him on a regular basis. It was Leekie.

Now, Leekie's dad wasn't exactly what you'd call a role model.

Leekie's dad was an original gangster before anyone talked about being an OG. He owned Mr. Cat's, a club by the projects in the Sixth Ward—and I had a feeling that Leekie's dad was a major pimp involved in things Leekie and I never really wanted to know about.

Still, I liked him. You have to grow up fast on the streets, and you need all the help you can get. So Leekie's dad was a valuable guide to me, and we would visit Mr. Cat's most weekends. Most guys weren't allowed in if they were carrying, but Leekie's dad would always let me keep my gun and holster behind the bar. He knew from experience that as soon as we stepped back out onto the street, we'd be at risk.

One night as Leekie and I were approaching the club, we saw Leekie's sister, Angela. She was about a block away from Mr. Cat's, with six guys crowding around her. She didn't look at all happy.

As we marched up to them, Leekie started shouting. "What you doin' fussin' with my sister like that?"

They turned to us. "Who you is?"

Leekie started cussing them out while I stared. They were all at least a couple of years older. They were wearing tank tops too, and I guessed most of them would have guns in the backs of their pants. It was clear within a few seconds that one thing would lead to another, so I pulled out my .38 and started firing.

This time there was no lifeless *click*. Six loud *pops* filled the air, and my shoulder soaked up the recoil.

I watched for them to fall, but nobody moved. We all stared for a moment, until it dawned on everyone that I had just managed to miss hitting six people with six bullets from close range.

I waited for the inevitable return of fire, but none came. They were not armed after all.

In a split second, everybody started running.

Mr. Cat's was close, and it was the logical place for Leekie, Angela, and me to go. But it was also in the same direction the six guys were running. So the three of us doubled back, hoping to take the long route to the safety of the club.

Five or ten minutes later, we were close enough to hear the music from inside Mr. Cat's when we saw the six guys cross the road ahead of us. They were all armed, and now there weren't six of them anymore. There were at least ten.

They saw us and started running toward us.

Leekie led us back down an alley, out of sight and into the first house we saw with a light on. We barged in, slammed the door, and asked the old lady inside if we could use her phone.

"Of course," she said. "Y'all gotta be careful out there. My boy's just been in here telling me that some kid's out there trying to shoot him. The kid missed. Six shots. Can you believe it? You stay as long as you need, y'hear?"

None of us knew what to say.

Leekie put in a call to his dad, and we waited for him to drive by and get us. In the two minutes we were waiting, I was convinced my heart was going to explode.

———

Later, when the club was quiet, Leekie's dad sat me down. He asked me what happened, and I explained as best I could. I was a little embarrassed about missing them all at point-blank range, so I talked more about how they would have probably backed off if they'd known I had a gun.

"I should have shown it to them first," I said. "I was too quick to fire."

Leekie's dad didn't agree. "No. Don't be wearing no tank top, letting everybody know you got a gun. Never show them that."

"Why?"

"If they see you carrying, they know you the one they need to get first."

It went against all the logic of the streets, but I had to listen to him. Leekie's dad had survived all the way into his thirties. He must have been doing something right.

"But here it is," he added. "When you do pull your gun, make sure there's smoke, y'hear? You pull it, you fire. Every time."

7 | DAWN

Girls were a big deal to us back then, and my main role model was my brother Reggie. It seemed to me that he had a new girlfriend every week, and even before Dad left for Florida, I was making my moves and starting to follow in my brother's footsteps.

Here's how it went. Leekie, J-Dog, and all the Four Horsemen—plus the guys who wanted to get a baseball cap and be a part of our little crew—would regularly take a trip to Bourbon Street in search of the ladies. We'd each put twenty-five dollars in the pot and then compete to see who could get the most phone numbers by the end of the night.

Reggie taught me well. He'd schooled me on the power of the compliment and the importance of a smile. He'd told me not to be too eager, but to also have fun and keep it light. I was the only real extrovert among the Horsemen, and I'd talk to anyone on those nights. The way I saw it, nobody was out of my league. If I got a return on my smile, I'd move on in and get the conversation going. Maybe even offer a little hug. There weren't many nights when I lost the competition for the most numbers. In fact, I don't recall ever losing. Not once.

But Dawn was different.

I didn't meet her out on the street, and I didn't talk to her because I was trying to win a bet. I met her one weekend when I was staying with Reggie at his new girlfriend's house. Dawn was a neighbor, and she was my age too. We liked each other from the start.

We started to date. I was serious about her in ways I'd never been serious before. It didn't stop me from flirting with other girls from time to time, but what Dawn and I had was real. We became close. Close enough to change my life. Close enough to change hers. Close enough to change the lives of some people not yet born.

8 | BEING RONNIE, BEING RONNIE SLIM

We were all making a lot of money, more than enough money to keep us in Air Jordans, guns, and alcohol. It was enough money to buy a car, but not enough to buy the kind of car that suited our status. That meant we were still without our own wheels. Now, stealing cars was fun, but sometimes—like on the days when we wanted to go robbing a whole bunch of different people all over the city—we needed a ride without the risk of police tracking us down. The solution was a hustle we called "rock rentals."

The deal was simple. We'd find one of our clients and have them rent a car and hand over the keys in exchange for their crack. It was a great system, and it allowed me to drive without all the usual adrenaline that accompanied a theft.

One day I was waiting in my rock rental up at the lights, Leekie in the passenger seat beside me. I noticed in my peripheral vision a car pulling up next to me, but it was Leekie who turned and stared.

"Ronnie Slim," he said, his eyes locked right, voice full of tension. "You ain't gonna believe who I'm looking at."

It was my mama, driving from one of her jobs to the next. And she was staring over at me. Right at me, her face drained with shock.

All my hours spent stealing and driving cars had made me confident behind the wheel. I was calm, too, able to think clearly under pressure. So I pretended as if I was just a regular guy out for a regular drive who had never seen this particular woman in his life. I nodded politely, turned my attention back to the lights, and when they changed, I pulled away calmly.

As soon as I was sure she was not following me, I floored it. I drove home like I had a hundred cops behind me. One of my cousins was staying at our house, and I begged her to cover for me and say I'd been at home all day when my mama phoned—which I guessed would be in about ten minutes when she arrived at work.

Shannon agreed and took the call when it came in. She said all the right things, but Mama still told her to get me on the phone.

"Ronnie, I know I saw you driving just now. You were with Leekie. I saw you."

"Mama, I been at home all morning," I said, getting ready to play my ace. "You know there's that guy Crawford who looks like me. He and Leekie been hanging round together. You must have got us two confused again."

That part of my lie was true. There really was a guy called Crawford living in the neighborhood, and he really did look exactly like me. We looked so similar and were up to the same kinds of things that I'd had to talk my way out of several conflicts with people he was in trouble with. And when one day we finally came face-to-face, it was like looking in a mirror.

Mama never mentioned the driving again, and I continued to pretend to her that I was the son she wanted me to be. In some ways I was. When I was at home, I was polite and respectful. I didn't cuss or do drugs or skip my chores. Even though my school attendance wasn't great, I made sure I always had a part-time job working in the kitchens of restaurants Mama knew. Sure, I got in a little trouble from time to time, but I made sure Mama only ever knew about the minor-league things like shoplifting. As far as she and almost everyone else in my family was aware, I was a good kid who could be trusted.

It wasn't difficult for me to maintain this act, especially as it helped keep things quiet at home. Mama assumed I was paying for my Air

Jordans and Starter jackets out of my restaurant wages. But I also liked being this version of myself. I loved my family, and I took way more pleasure from the money I sweated for at $3.35 an hour than the hundreds I could make in a couple of hours standing around selling crack.

The truth was that I liked being Ronnie.

I also liked being Ronnie Slim.

Whenever I finished work, I'd return home, change clothes, and leave the house as my other self, my gun safely in its holster around my side. I'd spend the nights with Leekie, J-Dog, and the others, running the streets, spiked on adrenaline, and keeping one step ahead of the police. Being Ronnie Slim was addictive.

To me, it didn't seem like I was lying or living two separate lives. Ronnie was the unprotected, unfiltered, unguarded version of me. Yet Ronnie Slim was who I had to be to survive.

———

It might seem strange, but of all the guys we knew in those days, there was only one in our neighborhood who didn't carry a gun, deal drugs, or involve himself in robbing or some other serious felony. This particular guy would hang out with us on the street, but the bottle inside the brown paper bag contained milk instead of liquor. When we reached the point of the night when the hanging stopped and the criminality started, he'd leave us. He was an athlete, but not just any level of athlete. He was so talented that he went on to play in the NFL and win a Super Bowl.

Think about that for a moment. Where I came from, the only way to build a future that didn't involve incarceration or an early death was to be one of the most gifted athletes of your generation. It took all the talent, all the connections, and all the determination of an NFL Hall of Famer to make it out of the Eighth Ward. For the rest of us, it would take a genuine God-delivered miracle to change our destiny.

———

I was able to fool my mama about my double life, but somehow one of my dad's brothers heard what I was up to. He lived in Texas, and one day when he was visiting New Orleans, I got a message that he was asking to see me.

I liked Uncle Michael. He was my favorite, and I hadn't seen him for a while, so I was happy to go visit with him. He greeted me with a hug and kiss and invited me to sit on the porch and talk awhile. He told me about life in Houston and how things were going well for him. He had just bought his wife a Lexus and had a brand-new boat, but he wasn't bragging. He was just being honest, and I was happy for him. And sitting there on the porch with my dad's brother, knowing he loved me and cared for me, it felt like I was able to exhale from the deepest part of me.

"You know, Ronnie, you really should come and spend the summer with us. We could spend some time together."

"I'd like that, Uncle Michael."

He paused. "And you know, I hear things about what you've been up to. You've been selling drugs, stealing cars, robbing people. Man, what's going on?"

I was lying before I even took a moment to think. "No, no, no. No way, Uncle Michael. I don't know who would have told you that, but it's a lie."

Uncle Michael let me keep on talking until I was all out of words. Then he paused, his eyes locked on mine.

"I understand what you've got into. I know where you at, Ronnie, but there ain't no life in that world you're in. I know because I've been there too. That's why I had to leave and go to Texas. And when I come back here, all my friends I used to run with, they all gone. All of them dead or in jail. I don't want that to happen to you. Man, I love you too much for that."

He stopped talking, and the silence rested heavy on us both. I didn't want to try to deny anything. I didn't even want to move from the porch. What he was suggesting—the summer in Houston, the prospect of a life away from New Orleans and all the dangers it held—captivated me. I wanted it more than anything.

In that moment, with Uncle Michael next to me, I could almost taste what it would be like to be free from the streets. And right then, I could almost believe him.

Maybe Ronnie Olivier might have a shot at living after all.

9 | "LET'S GO ROB SOME PEOPLE"

J-Dog was violent and out of control. I was combustible and ready to fight at the slightest provocation. But it was Leekie—the calmest, most clear-thinking one of us—who went to jail first. He took a gun to school, got arrested, and—since he had just turned seventeen—spent three months in an adult jail before, somehow, Mr. Cat—Leekie's dad—made the entire thing disappear. Leekie never heard anything else about the charge.

After his three months, Leekie came back to the Eighth Ward. Life hadn't been the same without him, and I was looking forward to seeing him again. But on the day of his release, he turned up with some guy beside him.

"This is my boy Duckie," he said. "I met him inside. Duckie, this is my boy Ronnie Slim."

I returned Duckie's nod and weighed him up. He was our age, average build, and looked just like any other guy you'd meet on the street. He carried himself just the right way: no sign of nerves but not too much confidence either. I just had this annoying feeling about him. There was nothing about him to dislike, but I wasn't ready to trust him yet. I trusted Leekie with my life, but trusting a stranger took time.

We had plenty of opportunity to get to know Duckie over the following weeks. He became a regular, hanging out with us most days. It was getting toward the end of summer, but the heat and humidity were way higher than usual. It was too hot to be inside without any real AC, too hot to be standing on a street corner selling crack, and way too hot to be getting in the kind of trouble that would have us running from the police. The weather had us trapped, and we could only wait it out. So Leekie, J-Dog, Duckie, and I spent hours sitting around on one porch or another. We talked, drank, smoked, and waited for a rainstorm to roll in, clear the air, and dial the temperature down just a little.

"Man, I'm bored," said J-Dog late one night. The storm was long overdue, and the temperature refused to move.

"I hear ya," said Duckie. The rest of us were too lethargic to speak.

J-Dog stood up like he'd been stung. "Come on. Let's go."

"Where?" Leekie asked.

"Round the neighborhood. Anywhere. I don't know. Let's just go rob some people."

Duckie stood up and took a step toward J-Dog. "Let's go."

J-Dog and I traded glances. We were both thinking the same thing, but it was J-Dog who said it first.

"Not you, Duckie. We don't know you."

"You don't *know* me?"

"That's right," I said. "Not yet, we don't. Not well enough for you to violate with us."

Duckie was mad. He stormed off the porch and went to stand a few feet away. That's when Leekie stepped in.

"Listen to me," he said, his voice low. "I trust Duckie. I've seen him inside. He's reliable."

J-Dog wasn't convinced, and neither was I.

"Okay," Leekie continued. "If he comes, we can give him the guns to carry. We get caught, the guns are with him."

One more glance at J-Dog. He'd softened, just like I had.

All four of us went out that night, but the streets were quiet. We found an addict that J-Dog thought he recognized, but the minute the guy saw us approach, he threw ten dollars on the ground and ran. It was too hot even for chasing crackheads.

Things got a little better when we turned a corner and saw a car parked up ahead, facing away from us. I recognized the vehicle instantly. It belonged to a guy who owed me money.

"Give me Nina," I said to Duckie, pointing to the 9mm.

I made sure the guy in the car was alone and didn't see me until the last minute, when I stepped by his open window and rested the pistol on the doorframe.

The guy looked at me from under his black Sacramento Kings cap, his eyes popping a little. There was no need for me to be the one to talk first.

"I got your money," he said. "Just not right now."

I lifted the gun up to his face and cocked it.

"I hear ya," I said, reaching into the car with my free hand and grabbing his cap. "That's why I'm gonna take this until you pay."

The rest of the night dragged on. We walked a little farther, looking to do better than ten dollars and a baseball cap, but nobody was out. The heat had suffocated the streets. Apart from us and a few cars, there were almost no signs of life.

On any typical night we wouldn't have looked so conspicuous as we walked down Eads Street. But there we were, sweating and strolling in the middle of the street, our limbs lead-lined with fatigue, when a police car turned on its lights and headed right for us.

I was in no mood to go hopping fences, but the adrenaline kicked in right along with the muscle memory. All four of us scattered that instant.

I was home within minutes. I changed clothes and took my position on my porch, watching for Leekie. Instead, I saw Duckie first. He came walking down our street, but just as he was about to reach Leekie's house, a cop car swung round the corner and took him in.

In the days that followed, none of us saw or heard anything at all from Duckie. It was like he'd just vanished. At first, we guessed he had hidden the guns before the police caught him. But as the days wore on and Duckie remained absent, we started to wonder. If he'd been released after his arrest, why hadn't he come back to return Leekie's gun? And if the police had found a reason to charge him, could we really be so sure he wouldn't rat on us to save himself? The law of the street says that anyone who rats deserves to die. That doesn't mean people don't talk to save their own skin.

I don't know how we found out, but we heard that Duckie had not been charged. Two weeks passed, then three, and still we hadn't seen him. Leekie tried to convince J-Dog and me that his boy could be trusted and that everything was fine, but neither of us was convinced.

So when Duckie finally came around one night in a rock rental, I knew he was guilty about something.

He pulled up outside Leekie's house. He sat there for a while, doing nothing but waiting. Waiting like he didn't have a care in the world.

Leekie went to the driver's side to talk to him, but I went round to the passenger side. I let him and Leekie talk awhile, but I didn't like what I was hearing. Duckie was acting like nothing had happened, which made me madder. And when he started laughing about something, I snapped.

I reached in through the open passenger window, pulled out the ignition key, and threw it down behind the front seats. Then I grabbed Duckie and started hauling him out. He was average size, and I was skinny, but I had the element of surprise on my side. He didn't fight back much, either, and by the time I got him out and pushed him onto the street, I was even more convinced he had done something to feel guilty about.

I punched him a few times until Leekie stopped me.

"Don't come round here no more," I said as he crawled back into his car and started searching for the key. He said something, but I didn't hear what. I was already heading back across the street to my house.

10 | DECEMBER 25, 1991

I spent all of Christmas Day trying to keep a lid on Ronnie Slim.
My dad had returned to New Orleans for the holidays, and even
though I was happy to see him and was enjoying his company like
I always did, a part of me wanted to leave the family gathering. The
longer the day went on, the stronger the pull became.

I tried to persuade my dad to rent me a car, but that wasn't ever
going to happen. It only led to more questions.

"You got somewhere you gotta be, son?"

"No, Dad. I just want to get out tonight."

"Why?"

That question I couldn't answer. There was no reason for what I
was feeling. I had nothing planned and no business to attend to. But
the streets were calling me. I couldn't ignore them.

———

It was about nine o'clock by the time Leekie and I stepped out of the
car and onto Canal Street.

"Be careful," said Leekie's dad before we closed the door. I thought
about pulling my black Georgetown Starter jacket back and revealing
the .38 in its holster but remembered what he'd said about not making
myself a target. Leekie and I nodded and set off into the crowd.

We had been walking a little while when I stopped, my eyes
locked on a group of people on the other side of the road.

"What is it, Ronnie Slim?"

"The reason I've been feeling like this all day."

"What? You trippin', Ronnie Slim."

"I don't think so." I pointed to a girl standing over by the gaming room. She was beautiful. Part of me recognized her, but I wasn't sure. "Look at her."

Leekie smiled. "Florida Jackson."

It took a while until it dropped. "The girl from school? I thought she moved away years ago. Man, she was fine before. She even more beautiful now."

"Uh-huh."

We crossed Canal Street, and I got my groove on. I locked eyes with Florida, gave her my biggest smile, and set the charm to overdrive.

I got her number and was giving her a hug when Leekie stepped in beside me.

"We should ghost. Look over there."

About twenty feet away was a group of ten guys, all looking over at us. And in the middle of them all was Duckie.

They started crossing the road, and I followed Leekie as he led me away. With ten of them and two of us, it didn't make any sense to get into it with Duckie—but I didn't like that we were leaving. If J-Dog had been with us, no way would we have been walking.

We were heading toward the Joy Theater when whatever movie was showing must have ended. The doors opened and a crowd of people spilled out. I looked back. Duckie and his guys were still following us. I stopped and stared at them, then I reached for my gun. If they knew I had it, maybe they'd think twice about starting something.

"No," said Leekie, turning me back around and guiding me through the crowd. "You fire your gun here, you might end up shooting Florida Jackson. Think about that, will you? Come on, we can ride the bus home."

We crossed back over Canal Street and headed for the bus stop by Popeyes. There were maybe eight or nine people waiting already, and Leekie and I blended in. We'd only been waiting a few seconds when I heard a bus coming and looked up. It wasn't going anywhere near the Eighth Ward, but as it pulled in, Leekie started moving toward the doors with the rest of the people.

"It's not ours," I said.

He glanced back over his shoulder. "We should get it anyway."

I turned back and saw Duckie and the others crossing over from the theater. I didn't want to be left alone at the bus stop when they reached it, so I decided Leekie was right. But I didn't want to push to the front the way he did. I would wait my turn at the back of the line. No way did I want them to think I was running scared.

I had one foot on the bus step when I felt a hand on my right shoulder. It grabbed my jacket, spun me round, and hauled me back toward the sidewalk.

I almost tripped but was able to catch my balance. As I turned, I saw all ten of the guys standing there. Duckie hadn't grabbed me, but some kid I didn't recognize did. Duckie stood right by him, eyes blazing. The other eight were standing back. If they were a threat, I'd deal with them next.

I pulled my gun. Shot the kid who had grabbed me first. Then I turned to Duckie and fired four times at him. I turned back to the kid and fired my remaining bullet.

I looked at the other eight who had been with them. They were motionless.

I leapt back onto the bus and looked for Leekie. He was sitting at the back, shouting at the driver to get going.

Someone else was shouting too. An old man, sitting up by the front. "They tried to rob you, boy. I saw it all!"

Other people didn't feel the same. I could sense their fear as I walked toward the back, the gun still in my hand.

The bus pulled away and turned right, then paused again. Everybody's attention shifted, and all eyes were locked on the sidewalk. We were looking at two bodies lying in a rapidly expanding pool of blood.

"Drive!" Leekie shouted from the back. "*Drive!*"

PART 2

SO HERE IT IS

11 | EVERY OTHER TIME
I'VE BEEN ARRESTED

I was only vaguely aware of the shouting on the bus. The driver had continued driving like Leekie told him to, but after a minute or two, he hit the brakes again and ordered us to get off the bus. Leekie tried to argue with him, but it was no use.

My head was full as I stepped out into the darkness.

First up, there was fear. Not for me but for my family. I didn't recognize any of the people Duckie had been with—not the kid I shot who'd grabbed my jacket, and not the other eight who'd stood back and watched. I had no idea how they would react or what they were capable of. I had to assume Duckie had told them who I was and where I lived, as well as about Dawn and where she lived. If they were going to come looking for me, I didn't want my family or my girlfriend caught up in the cross fire. There was no way I was going home or hiding out at Dawn's that night.

Then there was street law. According to the rules we lived and died by, what I had just done was nothing to be ashamed of. On the contrary, I had done what Leekie's dad had told me to—make sure I didn't just show my gun but fire it. I had sent a clear message: Ronnie Slim was not someone you ever wanted to mess with.

Every other time I'd fired my gun, it had either been empty of bullets or I'd somehow missed my targets completely. I'd shot at people plenty of times, but as far as I knew, I'd never actually *shot* anyone until now. I'd seen plenty of guys get shot and walk away, even those who'd taken multiple hits to the body. Guys wore their scars like medals. So I doubted that I'd killed either Duckie or the other guy, but I wasn't completely sure. *Had I just robbed two guys of their lives, or had I given them wounds they would brag about to everyone they met?*

Then there was the incident itself. *Was it an attempted robbery, or was Duckie trying to attack me? Had I acted in self-defense, or was I the aggressor? Was it a crime scene back there, or just another flash of street violence that would soon fade away and be forgotten forever?*

I had no idea what to think or feel about any of this, but I knew I needed to get off the streets, if only for a moment. I needed to clear my head and come up with a plan.

I went into a restaurant and headed straight for the bathroom.

The face I saw looking back at me in the mirror wasn't the one I expected. It was not Ronnie Slim, the man who could walk into a crack house without batting an eye or who could approach any girl he liked and ask for her number. No. It was Ronnie, the kid who cried when his dad left and who smiled at a sheet of perfectly solved math problems.

The tears started to burn.

"Who are you?" I said. "Who have you become?"

I was crying now. Sobbing, I saw in that mirror the person I used to be and the person I had become.

I was slipping through the cracks of who I was. I was powerless to stop.

———

I chose to spend the night at Kirt's house. He was a cousin of mine who lived nowhere near the Eighth Ward. I woke up early on December 26 feeling better. The confusion had lifted, and I was feeling calm. I was convinced both guys were still alive and that, eventually, it would all be forgotten.

Then I saw the local TV news.

The reporter was standing on Canal Street, across the road from where the bus had stopped. Behind him was police tape, and he was describing exactly what had happened. Only, it wasn't the same version I'd been telling myself. The reporter wasn't talking about an attempted robbery; he was talking about a murder. Of the two people who had been shot, one was in critical condition and the other was dead. Then a photo filled the screen. It was Duckie.

I was surprised, but a part of me was a little skeptical too. TV news treated what went down on the streets like it was bad entertainment, and I wasn't at all sure they were telling the truth about who was alive and who was dead. But I was curious. I needed to find out.

So I took a risk and talked to Alfred, my sister's dad. I told him everything that had happened the night before. His brothers were cops, so I guessed he might be able to give me some advice about what I should do.

"If all that happened the way you say it did," Alfred said after I'd given him my version, "then you don't got nothing to worry about."

"That's what the guy on the bus said. I was being robbed. It was self-defense."

"I hear ya, but"—Alfred frowned—"you want me to talk to my brother? It would be good to know you in the clear, right?"

———

It took most of the rest of the morning before Alfred was able to get his brother on the phone.

"They got a description, and they got a name," he said after the call.

"My name?"

He nodded. "I told my brother what you said about the guy trying to rob you. He says you don't got nothing to hide, so why be hidin'? He also says that the best thing you could do is turn yourself in."

I hadn't expected that.

I spent the rest of the day trying to figure out what would happen if I took Alfred's advice and reported to the police station. It was hard to know, so I ended up thinking about all the previous times when I'd been in trouble with the police.

The first was when I was eleven or twelve. I was caught shoplifting in a department store in Lakeside Mall and had been too slow for the security guard. I wound up being taken in a squad car to the juvenile bureau. The officers just made me sit and wait for Mama, who came and signed me out after an hour or two. Between her shouting at me in the car and my dad's belt when I next saw him, I had a strong incentive to stay out of trouble for a good while.

The next time I got arrested I had started dealing crack. One of my clients hadn't paid me for a long time, and I was concerned other people might do the same. I found the guy and confronted him. When he told me there was no way he was going to pay, I beat him up pretty bad. I assumed that was going to be the end of it, but the guy went to the police that same night. He showed them where I lived and pointed me out from the back of a squad car. A few minutes later I was on my way down to the precinct, my hands cuffed behind my back. Mama wasn't home at the time I was arrested, so I decided not to have her sign me out. I used my phone call to ask one of Reggie's friends to come and get me.

The last time I couldn't hide from Mama. My cousin Doddie was staying with us, and we were both pretty drunk when we went out that night. We saw a little white guy standing outside a liquor store, and Doddie got into it with him. I stepped in and stole the guy's hat when it was all over, and Doddie and I walked away. We were just about out of sight when four or five police cars screamed toward us and blocked our way. I got arrested for robbing the guy and was held overnight. The next day, Mama signed me out.

So everything I had ever experienced told me that if I took the advice and handed myself over to the police, I would be out before too long. It might take a night like the last time, or just an hour or two like the first two arrests. Either way, I was sure that as a sixteen-year-old and a minor in the eyes of the law, the police wouldn't have any interest in keeping me there. They'd shout and tell me how bad I was and try to scare me into reforming my behavior, but they wouldn't do anything to a kid like me. They never had before.

12 | LOCKED UP

There was no single, defining incident when I realized that all my assumptions about what would happen to me were wrong. There was no lightbulb moment when I could suddenly see my situation clearly. Instead, I spent much of that day telling myself everything was still going to be fine—even though there were so many signs that I was in real trouble.

As the first hour of police custody bled into the second, I told my story to the officers. They listened but didn't write anything down. It didn't strike me as odd in any way.

Everything is gonna work out just fine, I thought. *They ain't takin' this seriously at all.*

I found out that Duckie had survived, but the one who had grabbed me was dead. He was just fourteen years old.

Not good.

Three or four hours had passed by the time I was given a statement to sign. I read it carefully, but there was nothing in it about me shooting anyone. It was brief and vague.

So this is how it is. In the eyes of the law, I'm a kid. What they gonna do with me?

I still felt positive at the end of the day even when I learned I wasn't going to be signed out by my mama or anyone else. I was going to be taken to Conchetta Youth Center (CYC), the juvenile detention facility in Orleans Parish.

Okay, okay, I told myself as I was processed in and exchanged my clothes for the standard juvie jogger suit. *This is just gonna take a little more time. A little more time and everything gonna be fine.*

But then the reinforced metal door locked shut behind me. That was when everything really started to change. I stopped thinking about when I was getting out or how I was going to have some serious explaining to do for Mama. As I stood and looked around, it was clear I had more important things to worry about.

I was standing in one of the two dorms at CYC. There were around ninety inmates in each dorm, ranging from kids as young as twelve to others up to sixteen. That made me one of the oldest there, and I was grateful for that, because if one thing was obvious about CYC, it was this: the place was ripe for violence. What else would you expect when you lock ninety kids up in a single room no bigger than a horse barn?

Even though I'd never been to juvie before, the place felt perfectly familiar to me. It felt just like the streets did in the moment before the shooting started. Only in here, I had no fences to jump, no escape. All I could do was show that when the violence started, I would be ready.

I stood by my bunk and looked around. I recognized a few guys from the neighborhood, but there were plenty I didn't know. Some were checking me out, but I concentrated on the few who stared hardest at me. I made sure to return those stares with interest, not breaking eye contact until they did. It took time, and it wasn't going to exempt me from the fighting to come, but at least the strongest fighters might not take me down first.

Okay, okay. So we gonna be doing a little fighting in here. I'm ready. Show me what you got.

The real problem came later that afternoon before the lights went out and the fighting started. It was when I heard one of the security officers call out from the office that lay between Dorm One and Dorm Two.

"Hey, you," he said, pointing at me. "Over here."

He made me come closer to the office. Then he turned around and addressed another inmate who was standing opposite me in Dorm Two.

"You know about your friend who got killed on Christmas Day? The one down on Canal Street?"

The inmate nodded.

The guard stepped back and held his hand out toward me. "Any idea who this might be?"

The inmate stared.

The guard smiled at me, then turned back. "That's right. This here is the one who killed your friend. We got Mr. Christmas Day Murderer right here in CYC."

Okay. So this is different now. If I'm gonna survive, I might just have to kill again.

———

I was right about the violence. That night, Dorm One was a battleground. Not everyone was caught up in it, but it was impossible to ignore when two rival wards went at it. No weapons—just hand-to-hand combat. Bodies beaten down to the ground with elbows and fists.

And me? Well, word had soon got around of why I was there, so my reputation had improved considerably. For that night at least, I was safe. Nobody wanted to mess with me.

The next day, however, the danger returned. I was moved from Dorm One to Dorm Two. I didn't know why it happened or who made the decision, and I didn't waste a second thinking about it. All I cared about was the fact that I was now going to be sleeping in the same dorm as a guy who likely wanted to kill me.

I made sure he was the very first person I spoke to.

"That was your friend who got killed?" I said.

He nodded. His eyes didn't break my stare, but I didn't detect the same hatred I'd seen when we'd been separated by the guard's office.

"We straight?"

"We straight," he said. Then he turned away. I could almost smell the fear leaking out of him.

13 | I DON'T EVEN NEED A LAWYER

I have always learned best from observing other people. I figured out the importance of hard work from watching my mama sweating in all those restaurant kitchens. I got my flirting game from seeing my brother Reggie in action. Almost everything that made me Ronnie Slim—from stealing a car faster than anyone else I knew to swallowing my fear and never breaking eye contact whenever things got dangerous—I learned from watching and listening to the people around me.

So when I was in CYC and found myself with empty hours to fill, I made sure to study the other inmates and the system that held us, especially the guys coming back from court. Almost every weekday morning began with security calling out the name of anyone due in court that day. Most of the time I knew who was going to be called anyway—guys find it hard to hide their nerves when they're about to have their fate decided by a court full of strangers. But it was when they returned at the end of the day that I really paid attention, especially if they'd been sentenced.

What I learned was that even though we were all sixteen or younger, the sentences handed out were a lot harsher than I had imagined. Six months for auto theft. A year for robbery. One guy I knew from the streets even got juvenile life. That meant he was going to be incarcerated until he was twenty-one years old.

"Man, that's almost five years," I said as he sat slumped on his bunk. "How you gonna do that?"

He shrugged. There was nothing much to say.

After a few conversations like this, I was ready to admit that my previously held assumptions about getting signed out by Mama were way off target. Compared to what others in CYC were getting sentenced to, I figured that if I was found guilty, I'd be looking at anything from six to eighteen months. I didn't like it, but I had to face the truth.

———

It took a few weeks, but eventually my name was one of those called by a security officer in the morning. I lined up where I was told, and they put handcuffs and shackles on me. Within an hour or two I was sitting in a holding cell in the juvenile courthouse, just one of about fifteen juveniles appearing before a judge that day.

Apart from us sitting in the holding cell, people milled around everywhere. The room was noisy, and it was hard to follow what was going on. I'd never really tried to imagine what court would be like, but I had never expected anything like this.

"Ronald O—liver?"

I looked up and saw a woman standing in front of the cell, holding a file, and scanning the bench.

"Olivier," I corrected, walking over to where she stood. "That's me."

She nodded, and security came to open the cell. They led me out and into another cell on my own. My mom showed up without warning, as well as another woman. She was white, wore a business suit, and looked to me like she knew what she was doing. I had no reason not to trust her.

"I'm your court-appointed attorney." She paused, then looked at me closely. "So, Ronald," she said, leaning in even closer and lowering her voice. "You want to tell me what happened?"

I told her the whole story, just like I'd told it to the police.

"Well, if it happened like that, you're probably gonna beat this. Now, at some point today, your name's gonna be called. Then you'll stand up before the judge and be asked what you plead. Here's what I want you to say: *not guilty*. You got that?"

"Yes, ma'am."

And that was the end of it. She disappeared to talk with someone else, and I was taken back to wait with the other detainees.

The chaos and noise continued all day. I waited hours until I heard my name called. I did what I was told, confirmed I was who I said I was, and made sure the whole courtroom heard me when I replied, "Not guilty."

After that, I was told to sit down and return to waiting on the bench. It didn't matter to me. I was holding on to my lawyer's words: I was going to beat this.

Right at the end of the day, I looked up and saw Mama and Dawn approaching. They both looked upset.

"You don't need to worry 'bout this," I said. "My lawyer says I'm fine."

Mama looked doubtful. "I want to raise some money, get you a real good lawyer. Leekie's daddy did that for him."

"Mama, listen to me. From what I hear, I don't think I even need a lawyer. You save your money, y'hear me? Next time I'm in court, they gonna set me free. You just watch."

14 | AWAKE

On February 2, 1992, a little over a month after I arrived in CYC, I was told I was leaving. Not going home but to another facility nearby called House of Detention. HOD was a ten-story block in the middle of the city, and for those of us who had recently been charged as adults, it was to be our new home.

We were all nervous. It was one thing to be locked up in a dorm with ninety people my age and younger, but being locked up with adults was a whole other degree of danger. We young guys would be targets, plain and simple.

One of the other transferees was a guy from the Ninth Ward called Chico. We'd got on just fine in CYC and made ourselves a pact when we found out we were both on the transfer list.

"Whatever happens in HOD," we swore, "we go down together."

———

The eighth floor at HOD was made up of a long corridor, with two-person cells on one side and a TV room and showers at the end. Every cell had a toilet connected to a sink. There had been a big ward fight just before we arrived, so the whole tier was on lockdown. Each pair of inmates was only allowed out to shower in the morning and to collect their food at mealtimes.

Chico and I were put in a cell together, and that worked out just fine.

One of the other guys who transferred with us from CYC was

locked up a few cells away with an inmate who had been there awhile. He must have been terrified.

That night, not long after the lights died at ten o'clock, we heard the squeaking of tennis shoes on the floor in one of the nearby cells. I couldn't be sure at first which cell the noise was coming from, but when I heard the voice, I was sure I knew who it belonged to.

"No, man!" he shouted. "Leave me alone. Stop it. No." There was no fight in his voice. No threat. Only fear.

The squeaking of shoes continued, but the shouting died away, just like the lights.

The next morning when Chico and I were allowed out to get our breakfast, we walked past the cell. The guy from CYC was sitting on his bed, back against the wall, legs held tight against his chest. Eyes black and wide. The other inmate was lazing on his own bunk, eyes closed, looking like he didn't have a care in the world.

The whispers started up later that morning, and by lunchtime, everyone knew about the rape.

That afternoon, Chico and I were told it was our turn to shower. We walked out of the cell, down to the shower, and got undressed.

"You hear that?" Chico said.

"What?"

"When we walked down here. Those dudes whistlin' at us."

"No. But I tell you this. We gonna be listenin' when we get out."

Sure enough, as we walked back, the whistling started.

Chico and I marched up to the cell where the whistling was coming from and started cussing out the two inmates. One was stocky, the other tall. Both looked like they knew how to fight, but that didn't matter to us. We were ready to fight for our lives.

"Whenever these cells open, y'all need to be ready. You know?"

"We be breaking your jaws! You ain't gonna whistle no more."

We were raging—shouting, cussing, and staring daggers at them. They went silent.

Security hustled us back to our cell and locked us away. We were so jacked on adrenaline that neither of us could sit down. We were pacing and jumping up and down in that four-by-eight cell.

Later, when it was time for the two guys to get their food, they stopped by our cell and apologized.

"I don't care what you do with your mouth," I spat. "That's your mouth. But when we walk outta here, man, you better never whistle at either of us again."

"You got that," the tall one said. "That's on me."

The whole rest of the tier was silent, and I knew they were listening. I knew, too, that Chico and I had just won a significant victory. We had passed a test. We were no longer going to be considered easy prey.

———

My mama had visited me regularly since my arrest, and so had Dawn. But my dad? I'd not seen him since Christmas Day. At first I thought it was because he was back in Florida, but one day when I phoned him, I decided to ask.

"When you gonna come visit me?"

His reply was instant. "Oh no, sir," he said. "I'll not visit no prison."

And that was it. The conversation moved on. He was never going to visit me.

I cried myself to sleep that night.

———

It wasn't just the other inmates who were a threat in HOD.

I was sitting on my bunk one day, talking with Chico. I don't remember what I was saying, but I know I was saying it in my customary style. That is, every other word I used back then was a cuss word.

"Clean your mouth up, Olivier," said the captain of security as he passed by the cell.

I told him what he could do with various parts of his anatomy, as well as what I thought about his relationship with his mother.

Within seconds he'd opened my cell and dragged me out. Another security officer joined him, and together they took me across the hall to a janitor's closet. I was a little taken aback by it all, fearing what was going to happen next. But the two guys just started punching me, being careful to aim their blows at my stomach.

When I realized there were limits to what they were prepared to do to a juvenile like me, I went wild. I returned their blows with interest, and I made sure to aim at their faces. I connected once or twice, and they must have had a change of heart because they tried to drag me back out of the closet. I kicked the door so hard that it bounced back and hit the captain on his face, splitting his lip.

He staggered back and stared at me. The restraint drained from him, and he stepped in for another wave of attack.

"Stop," said the other officer, holding him back. "It's not worth it."

I was taken back to my cell, and again I was pumped full of adrenaline. And just like with the whistlers, everybody on the tier got to know about the incident. If there was any doubt about me before, now there was none.

Ronnie Slim was not someone to be messed with.

15 | JUST CALL ON JESUS

It took thirteen months before I got to trial. Thirteen months of being stuck in prison—first in HOD, then transferred along with the entire eighth floor to Orleans Parish Prison (OPP) on C4. Thirteen months of being taken back and forth to court, where I spent days and days sitting—chained and shackled—alongside a bench of other kids just like me, all of us watching and waiting, struggling to figure everything out. Thirteen months of hoping this would all be over soon and wondering why it hadn't ended yet.

During that time, when days melted into one another, boredom developed its own unique gravity. It was a black hole. Nothing could escape it, not even the surprise transfer of Leekie to OPP. He had been arrested for what went down on Canal Street, even though he was completely innocent and had nothing to do with it. It was good to see him, of course, especially as we were finally able to talk about the court case. But even then, with every conversation about the trial, I could feel my frustration level increasing. How much longer would I have to wait?

Early in 1993 I heard the trial was coming soon.

Leekie and I would be appearing at the same time, both charged with first-degree murder. Amid all the preparations, I could tell my court-appointed lawyer wasn't anywhere near as good as the private attorney Leekie's dad had paid for. Leekie had been visited regularly by his; I'd only ever spoken to my attorney in court for a few minutes each time. But it didn't seem to matter that much. We were both facing the same charge, and the judge and jury would hear the same evidence. They'd see that it was an attempted robbery, and I'd either walk free or be home before long.

Then the DA blew up all my plans.

He filed a motion to separate my trial from Leekie's and hold two trials instead of one. The judge was mad, Leekie's lawyer was mad, and I think even my lawyer might have said something too—but there was no way of changing it. The DA got his wish, and as far as Leekie and I were concerned, we were on our own.

Now, for the first time, I was nervous.

I wasn't worried that Leekie would rat me out—he'd rather cut off his own leg than do something like that—but I began to feel concerned about my own position. Without the added benefit of Leekie's lawyer arguing for our collective innocence, how strong would my case really be?

On the day of the trial in February, it took only a few minutes before I had my answer.

Without Leekie's lawyer, I was prey.

The DA announced he was calling four witnesses. My attorney was calling none.

The DA's witnesses gave conflicting accounts of what type of gun I used—one even saying I had a machine gun—but when it was time for my lawyer to cross-examine, she barely asked a single question.

When I took the stand, things really deteriorated.

For years I had been able to keep myself calm when everything was going wild on the streets. But here in the safety of a US courthouse, where words were the only weapons being used, I was as nervous as I'd ever been in my life. My mouth was dry, my head pounding. I was being torn apart by the DA, and there was nothing I could do to stop it.

———

"Bring him up here," the judge said later, looking at me. The closing arguments had been made, and the jury had left to deliberate. I took a seat in the empty jury box, right by the judge, and waited for him to speak.

He stared at me.

I was still nervous from the DA's questioning, and my mouth dried up all over again. But the judge's face broke, not into a smile but into something that was at least a little bit soft.

"You know what I think?" he asked.

"No, sir."

"I think you're gonna be all right."

With that, he stood up and went back to his chambers. And I was taken down to mine.

———

The air was still and stale down in the holding cell. It was quiet in there too, the first real silence I'd encountered all day. But I had no peace. My body could still feel the nerves from when I was on the stand, as if it thought I might need them again sometime soon.

And that's when it hit me.

This. Is. Serious.

It was the first time I'd let myself hold on to such a thought. Once I'd thought it, others followed.

I'm on trial for first-degree murder.

Twelve people that know nothing about me get to decide everything that happens next.

If they decide I'm guilty, I get the death penalty.

The brutal simplicity of it all was terrifying. Fear and panic started to rise within me. I stood up. I paced. I lay down in a ball and tried to glue myself together. Nothing I did stopped the fear. Nothing could defend me from the panic.

From nowhere, a memory butterflied into my thoughts.

It was of Mama, and we were just finishing up work together. My fingers were numb, and my back was sore from washing dishes. She'd spent just as many hours cooking—twice as many, given that this was her second job of the day—but she wasn't complaining like I was.

"You know, baby," she said as we stepped out into the night and I paused for breath. "If you ever have real trouble, the kind I can't get you out of, you can always call on Jesus."

The memory was brief, but the weight of Mama's words was immense.

I rolled onto my knees. Tears were instantly all over my face, pooling on the concrete floor. It was difficult to fight through the sobs and force the air into my lungs. But I was praying. Somewhere, from the deepest part of me, the words were screaming out:

Lord, if you don't let them kill me, I will serve you the rest of my life.

I don't know how long I stayed like that, crouched on the floor of the cell. But the sobbing was the first thing to change. It eased a little, then stopped. My breathing settled, and the air in the cell didn't taste so stale anymore.

I sat up.

Exhaled long and slow.

Inhaled deeply.

For the first time in my life, I knew that Jesus himself was giving me something. It was the very thing I needed most.

Peace.

I wasn't thinking about going home, and I wasn't thinking about the DA or my lawyer or even what those twelve strangers were discussing. All I knew was, for the first time I could remember, I felt calm.

I didn't know whether I was going to be released or sent to jail for a time. But I knew I was going to be okay. I knew it the way you know that when you're deep underwater, all you need to do is break the surface to be able to breathe again.

I couldn't explain how I knew, but I was going to be okay. Just like the judge had said.

———

An hour or so later I was back in the courtroom, waiting. It was late and everyone looked tired. Mama, my sister Penny, Dawn, the jurors, my lawyer. I was tired too. It had been a long day, and a long thirteen months. But at least it would be over soon. Everything was going to be all right.

The moment the verdict was announced, the only thing I was aware of was the sound of Mama screaming. It was a shriek. Pure pain. The sound of something tearing from way down in the deepest part of her.

I remember standing as the judge said something about me returning to court at a later date for sentencing, but nothing was really going in. I wasn't processing much.

Next thing I knew, someone was putting cuffs around my wrists. Then they were leading me out toward the exit. I could hear Mama behind me, crying, calling my name. But I did not look back. I couldn't.

It took me a long time to wake up to what was happening.

First, it was the uniform. As I waited in the holding cell, a guard gave me my prison clothes to change back into. Handing him back the white shirt, pants, and shoes that Mama had brought in for me, it was impossible to pretend everything was still all right.

"You know what just happened?" he asked.

"They found me guilty."

"That's right. You know the charge?"

I remembered the words I'd heard in the courtroom, but I could not repeat them.

"They found you guilty of second-degree murder. You understand what that means?"

I shrugged.

"It means you're going back to prison."

I thought for a moment. The words were forming within me, coming from deep within just like Mama's scream. Only when they came out of my mouth, my voice wasn't shouting. It was barely whispering.

"How long for?"

He paused. "Life. Nothing else they can do."

I was eighteen years old.

PART 3

LIFE OR DEATH

16 | ADVICE TO LIVE BY

April 12, 1993.

A date I'll never forget.

It was the day I was back in the courtroom. Standing tall, listening to the judge pass sentence.

"The State of Louisiana sentences you to life in prison without benefit of probation or parole."

This time the words were perfectly clear to me. No surprise, no delusion, no false hope. I didn't need anyone to explain anything, and I knew exactly what it all meant. It meant I was never going to be free. The rest of my life—whether it lasted eight years or eighty—would be spent behind bars. Even though I would not be killed in prison—not by the state, at least—I would certainly die there.

Because I had been found guilty of second-degree murder, I had been given a life sentence. Had I been found guilty of first-degree murder, it would have been a death sentence. Life sentence. Death sentence. Right then, I wasn't sure there was a whole lot of difference between the two.

I know Mama was there in the courtroom. Penny, Dawn, and some cousins and friends were there too, but I didn't pay them much attention. I couldn't. I had to be strong. If I'd let myself remember how good it felt to be hugged by Mama, I'd never have gotten up from the floor.

It was the same when I was led from the courtroom to the place where I was photographed and fingerprinted. One of the guards looked

73

at me kindly and tried to offer words of encouragement—telling me not to give up hope and to remember that things can change—but I didn't let his words sink in. I couldn't.

———

Now that I had been sentenced, I was transferred out of OPP. I spent a couple of months at a correctional center outside Baton Rouge called Hunts. Even though there was none of the violence of CYC or the cruelty of the guards I'd encountered at HOD, I felt lower in Hunts than I had anywhere else.

For the first time since my arrest, I was held in a cell on my own for twenty-three hours each day. There were no distractions or dangers to divert my attention—just me and the reality of what I had done to end up facing a situation like this.

I slipped back into memories of my life, watching them like old movies. I remembered the way everything was before I turned to the streets and the different person I became once I did. And I remembered all the times I had come face-to-face with death and escaped. Being shot at while I was stealing cars, being chased by the police and never crashing, running every red light—never wearing a seatbelt—and not once being involved in a wreck. Then there were the times when I had fired my gun and failed to wound a single person. The more I thought about all those situations, the more I wondered if there was something, or someone, behind them.

Eventually it started to make sense.

It was Jesus who had stepped in and saved my life.

But back then, that didn't leave me feeling good at all. If anything, I felt worse, because along with all those familiar memories came some feelings I'd never experienced before.

Shame.

Regret.

I had no words to describe or define them, but I knew what I felt. I was disgusted with myself, repulsed by what I had let myself become and by the sorrow I had caused so many people. I had brought shame on my family and robbed a mother of her son.

There, in my six-by-nine cell, with all the noise and chaos of thirteen other inmates on the tier with me, I was finally getting a clear look at myself. I hated what I saw. Unlike the time I stood in front of the bathroom mirror in the hours after the shooting, I realized in Hunts that I couldn't run away. I was stuck with the life I had created for myself.

———

Hunts was like an airport departure lounge. It served as a reception center where inmates were held after sentencing, while it was decided where they would serve the duration of their incarceration. Yet, for a lifer like me, the question of where I would end up was a formality. I knew exactly where I was headed. Everybody did. It was a place many considered hell.

At the time, every prisoner the State of Louisiana had sentenced to fifty years or more was sent to the maximum-security Louisiana State Penitentiary, otherwise known as Angola—one of the most brutal prisons in the country. Occupying eighteen thousand acres on the site of a former slave plantation that is bordered on three sides by the Mississippi River, Angola at the time was home to thousands of inmates who had committed the worst crimes possible. The stories of what happened behind its gates were horrific. Angola was a fearsome, terrifying place where violence was a way of life and sexual predators preyed on the weak. If you weren't able to defend yourself, anyone could take whatever they wanted from you.

And so, throughout my time in Hunts, Angola hung over me like a brewing storm. I could not ignore it; I could not block it out. Angola was always there in my mind, a constant threat for which I was constantly rehearsing and refining my survival plan.

I knew two things. First, I was determined not to end up as anyone's girlfriend. If someone showed any sign of wanting to take advantage of me, I would do everything I could to resist.

The second thing I knew was that if I had to fight—*when* I had to fight—I would be in a battle for my life. I would fight until I either won or died.

I was realistic about my chances. I would be going into Angola alone, with nobody to protect me. I was a young, skinny kid with a baby face. I looked less like an eighteen-year-old and more like a thirteen-year-old. I was going to be a target from day one. Weighing it all up, I figured there was a chance I'd make it, but that chance was painfully slim. I thought it was way more likely that I'd die.

I wasn't scared by the prospect of dying, but not because I was especially brave. There was just no point in allowing fear to take root in me. I'd learned the same lesson on the streets. Out there, fear is just another sign of weakness, and weakness will get you killed. The best thing I could do when I got to Angola was step into the unknown, face the fear, and fight. When my time came and someone showed even the slightest sign of wanting to exploit me, I would respond with everything I had. I would fight so hard that I'd establish an instant reputation for myself as someone to be avoided. I would make a statement—that when it came to fighting, Ronnie Slim was capable of anything.

My transfer date was set for August 23, 1993, two months after I'd arrived in Hunts. Between feeling low about the state of my life and preparing to face the brutal horrors of Angola, I hadn't put much energy into talking with people in Hunts. But that didn't stop one old-timer from talking to me. His name was D-Man, and we were in the same tier. He'd tried to strike up a conversation with me when I first arrived, telling me he'd served ten years in Angola, and I'd ignored him. But as the weeks dragged by and Angola inched closer, I figured it was worth the risk of talking to him if I could get some inside information on how Angola worked.

I wasn't sure if I was right to trust D-Man. His advice and insight weren't at all what I expected, but I took his lessons on board all the same.

"First thing is," he said when we talked at mealtime one day, "you look young. So that makes you a target."

"I know. That's why I'm going in there ready to die."

D-Man shrugged.

"What? You think I'm just talking?"

"I think you can probably do what you need to do to survive. But wouldn't it be better for you to know how to avoid that kind of thing in the first place?"

"I ain't scared. I ain't runnin'."

"Lil one," he said, leaning in closer, "you *should* be scared. That's why I'm gonna give you some advice, and I suggest you listen. First, stay away from gambling in there. Second, stay away from anything to do with homosexuality. And third, don't be playing and having fun with nobody. Don't joke with guys, ever."

I made a face. "For real?"

"For real. Those three things will get you in more trouble than you can handle. You stay away from them, and you gonna be all right in there. And remember, they got a lot of programs in Angola. You can get your GED, learn a trade, and do all kinds of things in there. You gotta graduate from everything you can."

I thanked D-Man. But I still went to sleep that night trying to figure out the best way to get my hands on a weapon once I was in Angola.

17 | FOR YOUR OWN PROTECTION

The guard took a long look at me, scratched his chin, and checked the paperwork on the countertop for a third time. I had been in Angola for two hours, and emotionally I was wired tight. This man—the captain of security in charge of the reception center where all incoming prisoners were taken first for processing—had the power to decide where in Angola I would be sent next.

"Eighteen years and five months," he said, not addressing anyone in particular. "That's what it says your age is."

His eyes switched back to me. "We don't want no problems here in Angola. Not for y'all, not for us. But you lookin' as young as you do, that's a problem. Plus, I read about you bein' a hothead. That's a problem too. So, we got ourselves here a pair of problems in need of a solution . . ."

Angola covers more land than Manhattan. The thousands of inmates held within its gates are all spread over seven different facilities, or camps. These camps function like separate prisons and are miles apart from each other. Even before I'd gotten there, it was clear that some camps had a reputation for being more dangerous than others. The captain was taking his time trying to decide which one would be best for me. It was like being back in court all over again, with me totally powerless and at the mercy of strangers.

"CCR," the captain said eventually, making a note on my file. "Best place for someone like you to get acclimated. And then, when you're twenty-one, we'll move you into General Population."

I didn't fully appreciate what he meant until I arrived and saw for myself that CCR—closed cell restriction—was an isolation facility. Single-person cells from which inmates were allowed out for only one hour each day.

At first, it wasn't so bad. There must have been more than one hundred cells in CCR, and each tier was a group of eleven cells separated from the others. It felt safe in there, as if the rest of the camp and Angola itself was a thousand miles away. Each tier had a TV on a stand opposite the cells, and during my one hour I was allowed out each day, I could exercise in the yard, have a shower, or play chess or dominoes with one of the other inmates through the bars at the front of their cell. I knew I was a whole lot safer in CCR than if I were in General Population, but even so, it didn't take long before I started doubting if I could cope with staying in isolation for the next two and a half years. For an extrovert like me, CCR was a slow, suffocating torture.

I was still feeling like I was going to explode when, in my second week, I was taken to the prison hospital for a routine checkup. While I was waiting, another inmate looked at me. I blew up in his face, cussing him out and threatening to hurt him just as soon as I was out of shackles and handcuffs. I'd hoped my aggression might act as an early warning to other inmates not to mess with me.

I also came to understand that CCR was not as safe as the captain had hoped. Angola's reputation for violence stretched into every corner of the prison, even the parts like CCR where inmates were supposed to be protected from danger. Within the first two months I witnessed how quickly violence could flare in Angola. The first happened when the prisoner in cell eleven paused at the end of his hour outside his cell and started pulling the TV off the stand. In less than ten seconds he'd ripped it down, smashed it on the floor, and begun hurling large shards of glass at an inmate trying to hide in another cell.

The second involved different people but ignited just as fast. An inmate pulled the fluorescent tube out of a light fixture and threw it at the guy in the cell next to me. The glass shattered, mixed with whatever gas was in the tube, and went everywhere, even into my cell. I hid my face under a T-shirt and hoped I wasn't going to breathe in any of the gas or glass.

Even though the classification officer had told me I might be held in CCR until I was twenty-one, each inmate had quarterly reviews. When my first ninety days were up, it was time for a visit from the captain. He placed a wooden table and chair in front of the tier and called out inmates one cell at a time. He asked me a few questions, but I didn't know I was the one who was supposed to persuade him that I was willing and able to move into General Population. It took him only a few minutes to deliver the verdict.

"You're gonna be in here a little while."

The news hit me hard.

A strange, lonely emptiness started to eat away at me. I'd always been a busy, energetic guy, even when I was in OPP, Hunts, and the other correctional facilities. But Angola was stressing me out. The walls were closing in.

Each morning began with an inmate offering me a broom, a mop, and a cup of bleach with which to clean my cell. I'd attack every inch of mine, sweeping and scrubbing until there was not a single speck of dust to be seen. While I was cleaning, I at least felt like I was doing something, but the relief I felt was only temporary. As soon as my tasks were complete, I'd start feeling claustrophobic and would spend much of the rest of the day pacing up and down in my cell.

The only real help was the hour outside the cell. I'd do a little exercise, take a shower, maybe exchange a few words with another inmate. I savored those times as well as the daily interaction I had with the guy who brought the cleaning supplies round. Even though they were always brief and never really about anything much at all, those conversations were like water in the desert. They kept me alive.

But I was conflicted. As much as I wanted to talk to people, I was mindful of the advice I'd received from D-Man in Hunts. I didn't want to get into anything I might regret later, so the only way to keep safe was to make myself as close to invisible as possible.

Between the bars on my cell and the fear of what might happen if I let myself interact with people, I was doubly trapped. Doubly locked away.

18 | THE DUNGEON

It turned out that when it came to doing something I would eventually regret, "later" came along a lot sooner than I thought it would.

I had been in CCR for about three months when my resolve failed. I made a friend, a Vietnamese guy named Tran who was a little older than me. I'd been careful and followed all the advice I'd received in Hunts, but I was desperate for something to hold back the loneliness that made my chest feel as though it was filling with lead.

Tran was on my tier, a couple of cells down from mine, and he loved music as much as I did. From time to time, I'd spend part of my one hour out of my cell talking to him about favorite artists, old tracks we loved, and how Q93 was the only radio station worth listening to.

When we'd been talking for a few weeks, Tran told me he had a Superadio and was able to listen to some New Orleans stations if he moved the antenna in just the right direction.

"You can borrow it if you want," he said.

"Real talk?"

He nodded. "Real talk."

As soon as I put the radio on, found Q93, and turned it up, I was lost. I closed my eyes and slipped back out of the cell, over the fence, and all the way home to New Orleans. In my mind I was in Club Discovery then Club Sensations, drinking a forty ounce of Olde English. As Rebirth Brass Band began to shout "Do Whatcha Wanna" through the speakers, I slipped deeper and deeper into my fantasy.

"Olivier!"

I opened my eyes to see a security officer staring at me. "Can't have that playing with no headphones," he said, holding out his hand. "Gimme that."

"What? I didn't know," I said in all honesty. "I just got here. You won't hear it again. I promise."

He frowned. "Okay. But next time, I got you."

And he did.

A couple of months later, I was trying to fix a Walkman I'd bought from the canteen. There was something wrong with it, and another inmate had lent me a little metal tool so I could unscrew the back to see what needed fixing.

I was about to open it up when the same officer appeared at my cell.

"Come here, lil one," he ordered. "Put your hands through these bars."

I did as he ordered and felt the cuffs bite into my wrists. With me secured to the bars, he entered my cell and picked up the tool I'd been using. He said nothing but stepped out, locked the cell, uncuffed me, and stood back.

Like a street magician performing a trick, he held up one of the cuffs and made a show of closing it. "I said I was gonna get you next time, didn't I?" Then, using the same tool I'd been using, he quickly unlocked the handcuff.

I stared back, confused.

"I know you don't know what this little bit of metal is, so I'm gonna tell you. It's a handcuff shim. And that, lil one, is the kind of contraband that earns you a ten-day trip to the dungeon. Pack your stuff."

In less than an hour I was taken from my tier. The dungeon was smaller than my previous cell, with a second metal doorway in front of the bars that ran across the front. If the last cell felt like a cage, the dungeon felt like a coffin. Instead of an iron bed frame, the dungeon's bed was a concrete shelf. Between seven a.m. and seven p.m., the guards removed the thin mattress. There was no TV to watch, no books to read, no cover, no blanket, no pillow. Instead of one hour, we were only allowed out for fifteen minutes each day, and that was only to shower. We were forbidden from talking to anyone else. Even the jeans, undershirt, and underwear that I'd been given when I arrived in Angola were taken away. Instead, I wore an orange jumpsuit that rubbed against my skin.

Those ten days, they really pushed me.

The loneliness, the fear, the claustrophobia—they all pressed down on me. Time slowed down and I could feel myself starting to slip.

I tried praying, but I didn't know how to do it. I recited what I could remember of the Lord's Prayer, but the words felt foreign to me. Since calling on Jesus the day I'd been found guilty, I'd not talked to anyone about what it meant to be a Christian. I knew nothing about it at all.

So I tried instead to replay my favorite memories—the cruises with Dad, good times with Leekie and J-Dog, riding the bus home from school or work. I'd play them slow, trying to recreate every little detail I could recall.

It would work for a while, but the effect was only temporary. Sooner or later, the darkness would claw me back.

19 | GENERAL POPULATION

After nine months in CCR, I was moved to the Main Prison working cell blocks—a part of Angola that looked a little like CCR, but where the inmates were allowed out of their cells during the day to work in the fields. We'd be given hand tools and taken out to tend crops while armed guards on horseback watched us. Apart from the weapons, it must have looked just the same as it did all those many years earlier when Angola was a plantation and the workers were slaves. At first, I didn't question it. After so long in CCR, I was a little drunk on what felt like freedom. But gradually I came to see how degrading it was to treat prisoners that way. Others felt the same, and by the time I left Angola, prisoners were no longer used for fieldwork.

There were some solid advantages to being in the Main Prison, like having access to the yard where I could play basketball. I could even have contact visits with my family with no screen between us, and I could hug my mom, take pictures, and eat with them. But I still wanted to get out and into General Population. In the working cell blocks, there was no access to any programs or the law library, which I was curious to get into. So, after six months, when a different officer placed his table and chair outside of my working cell and asked me how I was getting on, I was ready. I was polite and respectful as I asked him to move me out of the working cell block. I reminded him that since my ten days in the dungeon, I'd not had a single write-up for bad behavior.

He didn't look convinced at first, so I changed my approach.

"These cells are closing in on me," I said. "Please, you gotta give me a chance to go in GP."

He frowned. "You think you gonna be okay to take care of yourself in General Population?"

"I can take care of myself."

"And you ain't gonna get in no trouble?"

"I'm good. Nobody mess with me; I don't mess with nobody."

He paused awhile, then wrote something on the paper in front of him. "Just remember," he said when he finished, "out there in GP it's not *penitentiary*. It's *pay attention*. You understand me? Don't trust nobody in there."

———

Back when I was locked away in CCR, I had devised a plan for how I would approach General Population—a plan based on D-Man's advice and the instincts I'd honed on the street. On the outside I would appear quietly confident, calm, and self-assured, but inside I would be ready for anything. Ready to identify and keep my distance from all threats. Ready to fight and prove that I was not going to be anyone's girlfriend. Ready to kill and ready to die. As far as I was concerned, anybody could be a risk, so I planned to study every single inmate, trust absolutely no one, and always keep alert.

My new home was in the Main Prison. It was a sixty-bed dormitory with six showers, six urinals, six commodes, and zero privacy. It took only a day or two of being out there in General Population to see my plan was working—but it required one small adjustment.

The dangers were real enough, maybe even more real than I'd imagined. But I didn't need to search hard to find them. The traps weren't hidden down there on the West Yard in the Main Prison. They were open for all to see. In fact, the West Yard was nicknamed the "Wild Side." And wild it was.

"You hungry, lil one?"

It was my first night, and the guy in the bed next to mine was talking to me. He was a big old guy, two hundred pounds or more of muscle who looked like he could slap the teeth out of any man in the dorm. He'd introduced himself as soon as I'd arrived. He said his name was Delight.

I ignored him the first time he called over to me in the darkness, so he said it again. "Hey, lil one. You hungry? I got food for you."

"No. I'm not hungry," I said, my heart hammering in my chest. "I got food. Don't need nothin'."

I could sense Delight pausing, holding his breath, wondering whether he should try again. Minutes passed. I listened carefully, blocking out the noise of the fifty-eight other inmates, plus the security officer who was always there in the dorm with us, 24-7. It was only when I heard Delight's breathing grow slow and heavy with sleep that I let myself relax.

There were other tests for me in the days and weeks that followed. Delight tried to give me food a few times, but I stuck to my plan and told him no. Others tried to win me over as well, but I always stayed firm. I was determined that nobody was going to feel like they could own me. I remained thankful for D-Man's advice, and thankful for the fact that Mama and other members of my family were regularly putting money in my account. Even though my dad was still refusing to visit me, we talked every week on the phone. He gave me money too, and even though I missed him, I kind of understood his position. And at least the money meant I was able to buy zoo-zoos (candy) and extra food from the canteen. I made sure the guys saw me eating it.

The more I observed, the more I understood how things worked in Angola. The men—locked away for so many years—were desperate and looking for relief. For many of them, sex offered the distraction they craved.

There were three types of men in the prison. The guys like me who wanted to be left alone and just get through each day in one piece. Then there were the "bosses," the guys like Delight, who wanted sex even though they would never have said they were gay. Then there were the guys they did it with, the "girlfriends." Some were happy to go along with it and even embraced the role. I saw a few guys who had grown their hair long, wore skinny jeans and tight tops, and looked and moved exactly like girls. They'd sway around like they were mini celebrities, putting on a little show when they went in the shower while the bosses gathered outside and whistled and cheered.

Occasionally this caused problems, like the time when one of the bosses in the dorm across from me got tired of his girlfriend flirting with other guys. The boss took a five-pound weight from the gym and hid it in a pillowcase on his bed. When the lights went out that night, he beat his girlfriend in the head with the weight, then calmly walked to the security officer and told him what had happened. The girlfriend survived but needed extensive facial reconstruction. The incident was big news for a while, but only because from then on, the weights were all permanently chained in place.

Most of the guys who were being used for sex were the ones who had not been able to refuse tokens of kindness from people like Delight. They'd been cared for and invested in, and eventually they discovered they were now some inmate's girlfriend and had to pay it all back—usually in the gym where the security officers didn't patrol. They were weak and they were owned, and when their bosses grew tired of them, they might find themselves being sold to someone else for as little as a couple of cigarette boxes.

I never had to fight to prove I wasn't easy prey. Delight gave up on me soon enough, and the other attempts bosses made to win me over were easy to ignore. Other new arrivals were less lucky. A rumor went around that one of the new guys in the dorm had been taking a shower when a boss walked in, aroused. The new guy should have blown up, but instead he quickly left the shower. He was in danger. If he did nothing and tried to pretend the incident never happened, he would be the most vulnerable person in the dorm. The only option he had was to prove he was too tough to mess with.

It was quiet when he made his move, but I was watching. I saw him go to the microwave and boil up a container filled with water, Magic shaving powder, and syrup. Then he put on a work glove and carried the container back toward the beds.

The boss from the shower was lying down at the time, and he didn't see it coming. But he felt it. The boiling sugary mixture clung to skin like glue, burning deep, eating through flesh and tissue.

Unlike the incident with the five-pound weight in the other dorm, this attack didn't get spoken of all that much. After all, nobody was really shocked by the violence. This was General Population. This was the wild side.

They even let us keep the microwave.

PART 4

THIS WAY UP

20 | SPEAKING MYSELF OUT

It didn't take me long to figure out that violence was a fact of life in my dorm and that it was no different anywhere else in Angola. It also didn't take long to understand that of all the camps I could have been sent to, the Main Prison was one of the most desirable. It might have gotten a little wild at times, but the benefits of being there were considerable.

The upside was the facilities. Main Prison was home to the regular library, the education building, and the vo-tech schools. Between them they ran a bunch of different churches and programs—GED classes, Toastmasters, Lifers Association, Malachi Dads, substance abuse and juvenile awareness programs, and many more. Camps C, D, and F were miles away, and inmates in outer camps could not access the Main Prison's facilities.

Best of all, Main Prison was home to the law library. Even back in my time at CCR, I'd heard other inmates talk about visiting it and seeking the advice of the inmate counsel, a man called Stanislaus Roberts. He wasn't a lawyer by training, but he had fully immersed himself in the world of court transcripts and rulings. At the law library, inmates could read about other cases and work on their own. I figured that one day I should visit him too.

At first, though, I didn't care all that much about these extra opportunities. I spent most of my early months focusing on keeping myself safe and settling into the daily routine that would dictate the rest of my life.

Five thirty a.m.: Wake up
Six a.m.: Breakfast

Seven a.m. to eleven a.m.: Work

Twelve p.m.: Lunch

One p.m. to four p.m.: Work

Four thirty p.m.: Dinner

Ten thirty p.m.: TV off. Pay phones off. Lights out.

I was assigned fieldwork, which involved cutting grass, hoeing rows, or picking different vegetables. They'd stopped making the inmates pick cotton back in the eighties, but being out there underneath the Louisiana sun-bleached sky, working the line while armed guards looked on, made me wonder if not a whole lot had changed in a century or more.

Hard as it was, work was not the toughest challenge of each day. That came in those long hours in the dorm. The boredom and the need for constant vigilance ate away at me, leaving me more tired and stressed than any amount of hard labor.

I tried to distract myself just like I had when I'd spent those ten days in the dungeon. I pulled up old memories and tried to slip back into them as if they were a fully immersive movie experience. Sometimes it worked, but often I found it hard to keep my thoughts on track.

One night I was lying on my bunk, trying to wrestle my mind into my favorite Mardi Gras moments, when I remembered an incident that happened soon after I'd returned from the summer I spent with my dad in Florida. I was on the street, hanging with Leekie and others, when someone I knew only vaguely asked me where I had been for the last months.

"I was locked up," I had lied. "In juvie."

That was all I remembered, but the scene played on repeat in my mind. The more I thought about it, the worse I felt. Gradually, over the course of a day or two, I became convinced that in some weird way, I'd spoken myself into prison. I'd lied because I thought juvie sounded more impressive than hanging with my dad, and now I was experiencing some kind of payback.

These were the days when my faith was still so young and raw. It had no foundation to it—no wisdom, guidance, or structure. I didn't know about prayer or the Bible or why it's important to seek out wise people who can give good counsel. I was rudderless, changeable, and lacking in direction.

And yet, God was not. He knew exactly what I needed. And he knew exactly when I needed it.

Not long after getting stuck on the memory of my prison lie, I remembered some of the encouragement I'd received along the way. The judge telling me everything would work out all right. The guard at court telling me not to give up hope. The old guy at Hunts telling me to graduate from every program possible.

Then it hit me.

If I spoke my way into prison, why can't I speak my way out? What if I took every class available? What if I got my GED? What if I went to the law library, studied the law, and learned everything I could about my case? Could I work my way out of here?

And that's when I adopted a new mantra.

Angola can't hold me. I am coming home.

21 | THE VISITING SHED

God's grace shows up in all kinds of places. Especially when you're incarcerated.

Inmates in Angola were allowed ten people on their list of approved visitors. Mama was top of mine, and she visited me faithfully twice a month, often bringing one of my aunts, siblings, or cousins with her. I loved being able to spend time with Mama and give her a hug, but it didn't always go smoothly. It's not easy visiting a loved one in prison—being reminded of all they've done wrong while also knowing you've only got a few hours to spend together.

One day the tension was especially high, and she and my aunt got into a disagreement right there in the visiting shed. While I'd stepped out to the bathroom, they'd started cussing and shouting. Chairs were flying everywhere, and the blows were thundering down. It was typical for them but not at all acceptable for the Louisiana State Penitentiary. Mama and my aunt earned themselves a yearlong ban that day.

Not being able to see her in person for the long months that followed hit me hard.

Dawn, my girlfriend from home, was another faithful visitor. She'd been coming to see me ever since I was in CYC, and I'd watched her life change in that time. She'd had her first child while I was in Hunts, and she gave birth to a second when I'd been inside Angola for a couple of summers. Both times Dawn told me she felt bad about cheating on me, but I didn't see it that way. I was inside, and she was not. She had a life to live, and I had no right dictating what choices she made.

Besides, I loved it when she visited and brought her daughter. Jeanne didn't have contact with her biological father, and she always treated me as if I was her own dad. She would climb up onto my lap and snuggle in while Dawn and I talked. Those few hours we spent like that were always the highlight of my month.

But there was something even better to come. A gift of grace so precious I could never have imagined it.

We were sitting in the visiting shed one day, seven-year-old Jeanne on my lap. Little DeJá was about four at the time. She was sitting on Dawn's lap, her big eyes staring right at me.

Jeanne spotted her little sister staring and turned round to look at me.

"My sister wants you to be her dad too."

"Okay," I said, momentarily thrown off guard. "Well . . . do you think she could come over here and ask me herself?"

Jeanne nodded and beckoned to DeJá to come round the table and join us.

DeJá's eyes were even wider as she stood before me.

"Will you be my dad?"

My heart started a whole new beat. The air changed. It was like discovering that earth suddenly had a new moon. I leaned in. "What does your mama say?"

We all turned to look at Dawn. She smiled, nodded, and had a little tear in her eye.

DeJá looked back to me.

"Then the answer's yes," I said, unable to hold back the tears from mine. "I'll be your dad."

22 | THE LAW LIBRARY'S SECRETS

Stanislaus Roberts was an imposing figure. Six feet two with a two-inch Afro and a pair of the most intense eyes peering out from the darkest of complexions. He'd already served the best part of twenty summers in Angola and had successfully fought to have his death sentence overturned in 1976. But if the years had been hard on him, he didn't show it. His pursuit of knowledge was relentless. He was a force of nature, a rising tide with the power to lift all of us floating around beside him.

We called him Tony, and like so many of the inmates in Angola, he'd started his sentence suspecting he'd been badly served by the US judicial system. Unlike others, he had decided to do something constructive about it. Tony had dedicated himself to the study of law, and over the years he had built a comprehensive understanding to rival most law school graduates. He became Angola's inmate counsel, and the law library, located within the Main Prison, became his office. Hardly a day went by without someone visiting him in search of advice.

I was drawn there too. But for me, the law library's appeal wasn't just the breadth and depth of Tony's knowledge or the promise of justice. Something a little more basic drew me there. Tony's standing within Angola was so good that he was allowed to use a computer in the law library. Rumor had it that Tony had even taught other inmates how to use it.

I visited for the first time on a day when a thick fog squatted in the sky. Whenever visibility was low like this, the prison always cancelled fieldwork, not wanting to risk any of the inmates escaping (even though if anyone had been able to slip out of view, the chances of getting away were minimal). Angola was miles from anywhere, surrounded by the Mississippi, with a whole bunch of wild and hungry animals outside just waiting to sink their teeth into a wandering convict.

The dorm was too crowded for me that day, so I decided to see if the rumors about the law library and the tall guy with the piercing eyes were true.

"Sure," Tony said when I asked him if he really had a computer. "Ever used one before?"

"No."

"Can you type?"

"No."

"Do you want me to teach you?"

"Yes."

And that was all it took. From then on, I was fully enrolled in the Stanislaus Roberts School of Everything.

I started visiting the law library as often as I could in the evenings. First, Tony taught me about the computer. We started with the mouse and keyboard, then moved on to Windows 95 and WordPerfect 6.0. Within a few weeks I was able to begin searching the databases he had compiled of case law. There were thousands of records to look through, many with complete trial transcripts and judgments.

Like so many prisoners, my incarceration created a fascination with the law. I was keen to look up my own case but soon moved on to discover what I could about other inmates in Angola.

What I found gave me plenty to think about.

Right there on the screen I saw countless examples of racial injustice. There were multiple instances of two inmates being on the same charge but with the Black inmate receiving a harsher sentence than the white. I read the case of a white kid who had received the same sentence as me, but instead of firing six shots and then running away, he'd emptied his clip into his victim and then reloaded not once but twice more. Both of us were guilty, but my sense was that if the killer had been Black, there was no way he would have been sentenced with second-degree murder.

My hours spent staring at Tony's computer did reveal one area where white inmates came off worse than Black. Angola didn't separate sex offenders from the rest of the population, and most of those charged with pedophilia were white. I recognized the names of some of those men, and I had seen how, as soon as people knew what crimes they had committed, they became the most vulnerable targets of all. They were raped repeatedly, and for many of them, there was only one way out. They'd cuss out a guard, be written up, and be sent to isolation in Camp J, where they would hang themselves in their cell.

I also saw with my own eyes the consequences of the three strikes policy and how Blacks and whites were treated differently. I spent hours one evening reading about a Black guy who had been charged with armed robbery first, then theft a few years later. When he was caught with a rock of crack cocaine the size of a red bean, he was sentenced as a habitual offender and put away for life. That same evening, I read about a white guy who also had priors for armed robbery and theft. When he was caught with an ounce of powder cocaine, he didn't get life. He got five years.

"It gets applied selectively," said Tony when I asked him about the Habitual Offender Statute. "It's at the judge's, or rather the DA's, discretion. They don't have to use it, but it's a tool that helps them to actively discriminate."

In many ways, none of this was a surprise. The fact that the law treated crack cocaine differently than powder cocaine meant that Black drug users were far more likely to be incarcerated than whites. I knew, too, that inside prison, the inequalities persisted. As soon as I arrived in the Main Prison, I noticed that most of the best jobs—the gentle office jobs that didn't involve seven hours of digging in the field each day—were held by white inmates.

I said as much to Tony one day, but he didn't get agitated.

"Man, that's normal. It's how it's always been. But things are changing."

"Really?"

"Look at me. How many Black folks do you think were working in this law library when I first showed up here? Things are changing round here."

Tony was passionate about the law, but he also appreciated the value of education and experience. He encouraged me to get involved in everything that was available to inmates in Angola, from enrolling in a program that would allow me to get my GED to joining the Toastmasters public speaking class. He even got me—a former crack dealer who could make thousands of dollars in a single night—to become the treasurer of the Lifers Association.

I trusted Tony, even though my first experience at Toastmasters was a disaster. Like all first-timers, I was invited up front and given a random topic on which I had to speak for two minutes.

No problem, I thought. *Ronnie Slim's got this.*

I was handed a piece of paper with this title written on it:

ROCKY BALBOA

In the movie Rocky, he overcame a lot of things to be victorious. What have you overcome in your life to be victorious?

I stared at it. Let my brain warm up. I stared some more. My brain wasn't giving me anything.

I opened my mouth to start. No sound came.

I heard someone mutter something. I looked up to see twenty pairs of eyes locked on me.

I tried to speak again.

Nothing.
My mouth was rock-dry. My stomach knotted tight.
Someone was laughing.
And still I had nothing to say.

———

Thankfully, the next time I went to Toastmasters, I was able to speak. With that and every other challenge I accepted—each new responsibility I took on—I could feel myself changing. On the streets I'd never really experienced what it meant to be a typical teenager. Adolescence was a luxury kids like me could not afford. But here, locked away, I was able to do the very things I had missed out on at home. The clubs, the committees, the courses of study—they all combined to expand my mind and deepen my thinking.

And Tony was one of the father figures who guided me through it all.

23 | "COME TO CHURCH"

When I first arrived in General Population, I had a conversation with an old-timer that came out of nowhere. I was too busy paying attention to the dangers around me to think about it all that much at the time, but I never forgot what he said.

"You're gonna be preaching the gospel one day. No, no. Don't be shaking your head at me like that. I'm telling you the truth. You're a preacher man. I can see it in you."

I didn't say much in response, but I tucked the words away deep inside me. In the months and years that followed, those words would rise back up to the surface from time to time. I'd savor them, allowing myself a few moments to soak in the fantasy world where I was a preacher man. But I knew a fantasy was all it ever was. How could it ever happen? I knew nothing about what it meant to be a Christian, and even if I knew more, I was going to spend the rest of my life in prison. What kind of church pulpit could I ever hope to preach from?

———

"Come to church, Ronnie."

I looked up from Tony's computer and saw the man we all called Bishop Tannehill staring at me, smiling. He was tall and slender, but I'd heard his voice grow rich and loud whenever he preached. He was another inmate like Tony: a force of nature to whom it was almost impossible to say no.

But in my own way, I'd been ignoring him for weeks.

Tony's computer was bunched up next to a plexiglass window that separated the law library from the corridor that led to the Main Prison's church. Almost every evening I'd be sitting at the computer, and Bishop Tannehill would walk by on his way to church. He would pause briefly to tap on the screen and wave hello to me. I'd look up, nod, and then go back to my work. Every time I did, I had a strange feeling inside me, like I was instantly regretting something. I ignored the feeling though. Feelings weren't always to be trusted in prison.

This time, however, the bishop had taken it further. He'd arrived early, come into the library, and was now standing right in front of me.

He knocked on the glass and beckoned me to follow him. He spoke no words, but his message was perfectly clear—so clear that I heard it loud within me: *Come to church, Ronnie. And come now.*

I opened my mouth to explain why I couldn't, but the words wouldn't come out. So I just nodded and agreed.

That first church meeting was like open heart surgery. I'd walked in feeling awkward and a little on edge. An hour or so later, I left feeling like I was pumped full of light and peace.

From then on, I was hooked. Each evening I'd go to both places if I could: the law library and then church. I loved that I had a second sanctuary in my life. Under Tony's guidance, the law library was the place where I went to expand my mind, while the group of Christians led by Bishop Tannehill were the ones who helped me to grow spiritually. Both were great men of faith, and both took a keen interest in discipling me. Both men blessed me beyond anything I could have expected.

———

Bishop Tannehill was not the only person in Angola with a big vision for transforming inmates' lives. There were others, both inmates and staff, who had taken bold and courageous steps to help turn things around. A lot had changed in the prison over the years, and the scope of the Main Prison church had expanded significantly, even to the point where they held regular banquets for certain inmates and their visitors. If you were a church member and could afford the ten-dollar fee, you could invite someone from your visitor list to come along for a church service followed by a really good meal in the visiting shed.

I threw myself into every available opportunity. I loved being busy and being able to spend time around men I could look up to and learn from. When it came to my faith, I was a sponge, soaking up everything that came my way. I was also a toddler, learning to walk and talk and beginning to use the muscles that had previously been asleep. I was a novice, learning from my mistakes.

At least, I was. Until it all went wrong.

———

I'd signed up to be a part of the juvenile awareness program, and we'd spent weeks rehearsing for a show to perform in front of visiting kids. I was appearing in a few skits, and on the night before our performance, I was feeling nervous. I was trying to calm myself, lying on my bed in the dorm, focusing on my lines, and trying to ignore the twisted ball of fear that was knotting itself up inside me.

I was twenty-one and had been in Angola for three summers—long enough by then to have established myself. I was still always careful to stay away from gambling and anything to do with homosexuality, but I didn't feel the need to worry about joking around with people, even though that was something I'd been warned about. So I'd made a few friends in the dorm, and we'd play around a little bit like we'd have played about on the street. We joked a lot, and from time to time it got a little physical—a butt tap here or a shoulder barge there.

Nothing ever came of it. It was just a safe way for us to relax and let our guard down.

One of the guys I hung out with was from the Seventh Ward, and on the evening I was trying to rest up and get calm before the juvenile awareness skits, he decided it was a good time to rile me up.

"Don't do that," I said the first time he walked by my bunk and tapped the book I was reading.

He came back a few minutes later.

Slap. My book was out of my hands and on my lap.

"Man, I'm telling you, it ain't the right time right now. Don't play with me."

He looked at me, face locked solid. Then he shrugged, smiled, and walked away.

I knew what the right thing to do was. I should just lie back, calm myself down, and let it ride. But I couldn't let it ride. If he wasn't going to listen to my two warnings, maybe he wasn't respecting me.

Instantly, the old Ronnie Slim came raging back.

I stood up, walked over, and shoved the guy off-balance. Then followed it up with a quick combination.

He took my punches, gathered himself, and grabbed me tight. Before we could really complete this challenge, the security officer rushed over, broke us up, and somehow held me to the ground.

Lying there, my face pressed up against the cold, painted floor, I started to feel nauseous. I was hit by the sudden, suffocating realization of the consequences of what I'd just done. Rules were rules, and I'd just broken one of the most important ones in the prison: Anyone caught fighting would receive an immediate write-up. As the aggressor, I'd be sent away from the Main Prison to another camp, so that little shove-and-punch combination had cost me almost everything I valued in Angola. There would be no more Main Prison dorm. No more law library. No more going to church every day. No more Toastmasters. No more juvenile awareness program. No more Lifers

Association. No more feeling like I was growing in strength and character day by day. No more following the advice I'd received in Hunts about graduating from every program possible. No more hope of one day, somehow, getting myself out from this place. No more Bishop Tannehill. No more Tony.

24 | CAMP D IS A VIOLENT HELL

Camp D is about five miles away from the Main Prison, but it felt to me like it was in another time zone altogether. While inmates were allowed to make the journey back to the Main Prison for family visits and callouts—preapproved appointments elsewhere in the prison, such as the hospital—there was no access to the regular, weekly programs and facilities I'd relied on. Just as I feared, the law library, Bishop Tannehill's church, and everything else I had come to depend on faded from my life. The only plan I could think of was to wait the standard ninety days until my review came around, then argue my case for being returned to Main Prison. If my experience getting out of CCR taught me anything, it was that leaving Camp D would be a struggle.

Camp D did offer some programs, but the range was small by comparison. They had a church, but as far as I could tell, it was nothing like the exciting, vibrant community Bishop Tannehill had nurtured. But the real problem with Camp D wasn't the lack of opportunity or the boredom that spread like fungus as a result. It was the violence.

You could feel it hovering in the atmosphere when you woke up. Guys would get into it and start brawling even before breakfast. The smallest disagreement would escalate within seconds to the level where at least one person would end up with life-altering injuries. The kind of incident that happened once a year in the Main Prison—like the time the guy attacked his girlfriend with the five-pound weight—happened at least every month in my new home. People would improvise weapons out of anything, from a sock full of padlocks to a knife made from a piece of iron. There was zero trust between inmates.

I was on high alert all the time. Once more, I was back at the beginning, watching everything and everyone like my life depended on it.

Even the guards were affected. Back in Main Prison, a few guards had reputations for being tougher than others, but in Camp D, a bunch of them were just plain cruel. One guy—a super scrawny dude—would regularly go out of his way to degrade and humiliate inmates. Whenever we came back from a work detail or a callout, we were always checked to make sure we weren't smuggling anything back into the dorm. Most guards would just pat you down and check your pockets, but Mr. Skinny would rarely be satisfied with that. He'd make you strip all the way down, lift up your testicles, wiggle your toes, bend over, and cough. It was obvious he got a buzz from it, but what could we do?

One day, not too long after I arrived at Camp D, someone decided that doing nothing wasn't okay anymore. So a guy went up and hit Mr. Skinny. Then he hit him hard again. And again and again. The dorm instantly ignited in a firestorm of people shouting and cheering. A couple of other guards came running in and broke it up quickly, but blood was everywhere.

"That's why I didn't get you myself," one guy near me yelled as the guard was carried out of the dorm. "I knew someone else was gonna get you!"

It was a rare moment of unity in Camp D. The next day the inmates were back to fighting among themselves.

———

The church Bishop Tannehill had welcomed me into was a reflection of the energy and opportunity that characterized the Main Prison. The church in Camp D was an equal reflection of what it took to survive in those surroundings. The brothers there were serious guys, quietly going about life.

There was one guy who came by my bed when I first arrived in Camp D. Toward the end of a long day, I was trying to release some of the adrenaline from my system after being on high alert in this new environment. I was lying back on my bed, hoping that eventually I might be able to get some sleep. But the brother just hovered beside me, Bible in hand, a concerned look on his face.

"Man, I don't want to talk to you right now," I said.

He left, but the next evening, he was back—Bible and frown on display as he crouched down next to me and asked how I was doing.

"I don't want to talk with you," I said. "I'm not interested."

He nodded and shuffled off.

Next evening, he was there again.

And the next. And the next.

Eventually I gave in and told him I'd come to church.

"That's good," he said. "I knew you would eventually."

"How come?"

"The Lord had me prayin' for you ever since you got here. Every morning, from four to five, I been wakin' up, prayin' for you. That's why I keep on comin' back here. It's what the Lord wants."

25 | RUNNING EPS

One thing all lawyers agree on is this: When you're locked up inside, don't talk about your case to anybody. Ever. Don't talk about what you really did, what you got away with, or the lies you told to get there. You might think you can trust people, but if there's one thing you can count on, it's that a desperate inmate won't think twice about betraying you if he thinks it will help him get out. That makes talking a risk.

Trouble was, there weren't too many options aside from talking in Camp D. Trying to figure out what to do in the six and a half hours between work ending and the lights going off was a struggle. The TV room was often where the fights started, so all I ever really could do to pass the time was hang back in the dorm with the other guys who just wanted a quiet life. The solution was to share stories and memories from when we were out on the street, and we often showed each other photos as we talked. We called this "running eps"—short for episodes—and we kept the stories focused on the good times, the times that made us laugh. Naturally, we talked a lot about girls.

I put my photos in an album and would happily flip through the pages and show people the pictures from my past. Family cruises with Dad, those big old barbecues where people spilled out onto the street, good times with Dawn, even a few shots of J-Dog and Leekie and me standing around in our FOG caps, reminding everyone that we were the Four Horsemen, the kings of the world.

Most of the time, those photos would bring smiles. They'd help me feel connected to my past, to feel as though my life was not over. When I slipped into those memories, Camp D melted away.

At times the memories were not so sweet, like the time I received a visit from Mama. After we hugged and sat at the table, she said, "I got some bad news for you. One of your boys got killed."

"Who?"

She slid me a folded newspaper clipping, a two-by-four-inch column from the Obituary section. It was J-Dog. He'd become a major drug dealer, and someone had decided they wanted him dead. Some guys surrounded his house and shot it up when J-Dog was inside with his girlfriend and baby daughter. The police found him lying on his back with a gunshot wound to his chest, an AK-47 in his hands. Amazingly, his pregnant girlfriend and unborn child survived a bullet wound, and his three-year-old daughter wasn't harmed at all. I was shocked, and for perhaps the first time, I saw my old life clearly. But a part of me wanted to get out of Angola so bad. I wanted to retaliate. I couldn't believe J-Dog was killed like that.

———

I wasn't the only inmate to come from my neighborhood. Eric Matthews was a little older than me, but we knew a few of the same people. We always had a lot of good eps to run. We'd talk about some of the characters we both knew, plus girls we'd liked. But Eric had never been as wild on the streets as I had. He'd been a gifted tae kwon do fighter and had gone on to serve in the military. For a while it appeared he was one of the rare few who had been able to escape the Ninth Ward with both his life and his freedom intact. But one night had changed everything. A single moment when he'd lost control. He was sentenced to spend the rest of his life in prison, just like me.

When Eric and I were in the Main Prison, we were always either at church or in the regular library, and it was clear he and I had a similar appetite to get involved in as much as possible with programs that would enrich us. Our conversations reflected that, and we talked freely about the struggles we were going through and the solutions we had found that worked.

The more we talked, the deeper and more personal our conversations became. It was hard to spot at the time and hard to define what was going on, but eventually it happened. We broke the essential advice that both our lawyers had given us. We talked about our cases.

It was just a regular day. Work was over, and we were sitting alone in a classroom in the education building, killing time like we always did. But somehow, we started talking about what had happened the night we both became killers.

Our voices were hushed, and the words came slow as we talked. This was no ep that we were running—not a story told for entertainment or amusement. As I started talking about Christmas night on Canal Street and feeling the kid's hand on my shoulder as I stepped onto the bus, this was a confession.

I had spoken with my lawyer and my sister's uncle (the police officer) about the shooting, but I'd never told anyone before what really happened. I'd always filtered the story, shading things this way and that to suit my purpose. I'd made myself seem like the victim and my victim like the aggressor. But as I talked with Eric, I had no filters. There was only the truth. I told him everything, even though some words stung my throat like bile.

When I was done, Eric spoke. His voice was quiet and slow, breaking in parts. It cost him just as much as it did me to talk like this.

When we both were finished, we sat in silence for a while. But it wasn't the end. It was only a pause. Our words changed from confession to prayer.

We prayed for forgiveness, for God's mercy and love to flood us both. We prayed for hope to replace despair, for peace to grow where shame had taken root. We prayed for a new beginning, that each of us would know what it meant to follow Jesus more closely with our steps.

There were tears from both of us that day.
Regret. Pain. Sorrow. We cried it all out.
But we cried in a lot of stuff as well.
Hope. Forgiveness. Gratitude.

26 | CUSSING

I don't want to brag about this too much, but I was a pretty good cusser. I used more cuss words than anyone I knew, and I could string together whole paragraphs with nothing but profanity, hooking up new combinations that the people listening would never even have thought possible. Most of the time, I barely knew I was even doing it.

After the trial, not much changed about my vocabulary choices. I'd had that moment in the holding cell when I'd promised to follow God if my life was spared, and I meant it too. But those cuss words seemed wired into me. They were a part of my mother tongue, my birth language. For a long time, I barely noticed that I was still talking that way. But gradually, as I spent more time in church and more time around Christians, I started to hear myself. I was a cussing Christian, and it didn't seem right.

By the time I was sent to Camp D, I'd had enough. I was determined to deal with the issue and clean my mouth up. I wasn't alone: a bunch of us who attended church in Camp D were feeling the same.

Our first plan sounded so simple.

"Any guy gets caught cussing, he has to do ten push-ups right there, right then."

I tell you, I was on the floor all day long. My arms were tired, my chest hurt, and my mouth still sounded like a sewer.

"Okay, how about this," said a guy called Steve when we were trying to figure out a better option. "Anyone gets caught cussin', another guy can slap him on the back of the neck."

That plan lasted less than an hour, and we only narrowly avoided getting a write-up and sent to the dungeon for starting a brawl.

We tried other ideas, too, but nothing worked.

Then I tried praying.

"Lord, I need you. I thought I could just stop, but I can't. Man, you're gonna have to help me with this."

I was lying on my bed at the time, doing what I normally did in the last few moments before the lights went out. I had my Walkman on my chest and my little orange-foam headphones on my ears. I was about to press Play and start listening to Master P, a New Orleans artist who rapped about the streets and whose brother C-Murder was later locked up in Camp J.

What are you doing? The voice came out of nowhere. Loud and clear, I heard it as if Master P himself was speaking. But I hadn't pressed Play. And even if I had, Master P never spoke four words without cussing.

I pulled my headphones off and looked around, assuming that whoever had just spoken to me had been standing right by my head. There was nobody there.

I lay back and put the headphones on again, ready for a little more Master P rapping about ghetto heroes.

What are you doing?

The voice was louder this time, and there was no mistaking the criticism that was loaded in the words. Whoever was talking to me was not impressed.

I sat up again. Looked around. Nobody there.

I eased myself back onto my bed, about to plug in again, but I could not settle. Because in that moment, without a shadow of a doubt, I finally understood what was wrong. I knew precisely whose voice I'd just heard. And I knew I couldn't listen to that kind of music anymore.

At the time I had a brother-in-law who worked at Peaches Record

Store down on Gentilly and Elysian Fields. He knew what I liked, and he was always sending me cassette tapes of the latest rap releases. I had a whole box full of these tapes, and I'd lend them out to people from time to time.

I sprung Master P from my Walkman, grabbed the box that contained my extensive musical library, and tried to figure out what I should do next. Sell the lot or give them away?

Then the voice came back.

If it's not good for you, what makes you think it will be good for them?

So I walked over to the garbage can. I started pulling the tape out from each cassette, filling the can with a mess of shiny black ribbon.

"Ronnie?" One of my friends had noticed what I was doing and was staring at me, stunned. "You trippin'?"

"I'm straight," I said. "Never been better."

When the box of tapes was unspooled in the can, I went back to my bunk and reached into my locker. A few seconds later I was back at the can, ripping up my collection of porn magazines. This time more howls of protest rang out, but I ignored them. There was only one voice I wanted to listen to.

That night, even before the lights went out and the dorm was dragged into darkness, I was asleep—deep asleep, as if I'd not slept for a long, long time.

And when I woke up, I felt great. I felt alive. I felt like a new person.

The feelings remained all day. The next day too. After that, reality set back in a little, and a few normal life challenges and everyday distractions took the edge off my buzz. But I still felt as though something had shifted in me.

It's hard to see the big picture when you're in it, and it took me about three weeks to work it out. Three weeks and a conversation with Steve and Z-Man, two brothers I went to church with.

"Man, you ain't been the same," Steve said. "You changed."

He was right, and for the first time I realized that from the moment when I prayed and threw away my cassettes and porn, I'd not uttered a single cuss word.

And I still haven't today.

27 | COULD SHE FORGIVE ME?

The change to the way I spoke was big, but what it revealed to me about God was even more ground-shaking. For the first time in my life, I realized that my own efforts and willpower were not enough to change me. The transformation I wanted—the kind that would really last—could only come from God. I needed him to take away the desire to swear. I needed him to change my appetite and tastes so I would no longer want to behave like I did. I needed him, period. I couldn't do it on my own.

Slowly, I began to see myself for what I was: a newborn Christian. And like all newborns, I looked like what I had come out of. Even though it had been about three years since the moment of my spiritual birth back in the holding cell, I'd spent much of that time just trying to survive in prison. But things were different now. I was as safe as I was ever going to be in Angola, and I was discovering a fresh appetite for God's transformation in my life. There was still a lot of mess to be cleaned off me—old habits left over from my past—but now I was full of faith that God could step in and fix me up.

I chose to put myself in places where I could grow. I joined an intercessory prayer team. I spent as much time as I could in the Christian library in the Main Prison. I slowly built up my music library with worship tapes. I took a notebook to church so I could study the sermons in the days that followed. I wanted to feed on things that would be good for me, so I signed up for whatever Bible study or discipleship course was available—then, when I was there, I made sure to always ask questions and listen carefully to the answers.

The more I set my focus on the things of God, the more of them I wanted in my life. It was a strange kind of hunger, not at all like the desperate cravings I used to feel when I was running wild. Back then, the more I gave in to my appetites for drink and women and adrenaline, the less satisfied I felt. But now I was experiencing the paradox of being deeply satisfied by what God was doing in my life, while at the same time wanting more of it.

―――――

Two years into my time at Camp D, four summers into Angola, I decided to accept that I was there for good and stop wishing I could be back in the Main Prison. I'd come to see the upside to my being in Camp D: the lack of programs and facilities cut down on the possible distractions, and the constant threat of violence kept me dependent on God.

Once I'd accepted that I was likely going to be in Camp D for a long, long time, I did something I'd never have considered when I first arrived. I applied for a job.

Having a job locked you in your camp and made it harder for you to be transferred. But it was another way of showing the Angola authorities that you were making good choices with your time. Plus, the work was paid. Even though the rate was just four cents per hour, I welcomed it. When Mama had been banned from the visiting shed, those $200 monthly deposits into my account dropped off. Even when the ban was over and she could visit again, the money never quite reached the same levels as before. I was at peace with it all, but I still needed cash.

I took a job working in the same place where my Angola journey began: CCR. I was an orderly, serving the food trays and doing the morning rounds with the mops and bleach for the inmates who, like me, were locked up for their own safety.

I hadn't been doing the job long when I encountered a problem. I was passing out food one afternoon, starting with the special diet drinks various inmates needed, when I spilled some tomato juice.

"I'm sorry," I said as I wiped the bars. The inmate wasn't impressed. He sat there, glaring at me, then returned to the novel he was reading.

The next day I was doing the same task: passing the plastic cups full of juice through the bars. My mind was wandering, and I made the same mistake again—only this time, the drink spilled on the guy's floor as well. And this time, he didn't stay silent.

"You doin' this on purpose?"

"No," I said, trying to mop up the worst of the spill before it spread. "I'm sorry. I really am."

He didn't take my apology. Instead, he started cussing and yelling, calling me all kinds of things.

I paused and stepped back, looking him in the eye. I was calm, a lot calmer than he was. "Now, you know that if you wasn't in that cell and we were outside, you wouldn't talk to me like that. Why we gotta go there?"

He reached through the bars to slap me in the face. Instinct made me swerve to avoid the slap. As he grazed my cheek, I grabbed his arm.

Now, I can handle anybody cussing me out and saying whatever they want, but people laying a hand on me just gets me wild. Something ignites inside me, and I get mad. The way I always saw it, I got all rights and privileges to hurt you and hurt you bad if you touch me first. Then you'll never think about doing something like that to me again.

So as I was standing there, his arm sticking out through the bars, held tight in my right hand, instinct told me what to do. One swift, double-handed pull of his arm backward against the bar would snap his bones like a dead branch.

The instinct was there inside me. But so was the voice.

Let him go.

Just like the time I was about to listen to Master P on my Walkman. Loud and clear.

Let. Him. Go.

So I did. I backed off. I walked away and continued with my rounds.

Inside, I was rejoicing. I was celebrating like I'd just been released. I was praising God, nothing but joy and gratitude in my heart.

The next week I was told I would be changing jobs. I hadn't put in a request for a move, but someone somewhere had decided that my short time in CCR was over. I had no idea why or whether it had anything to do with the incident. But when I found out where I was going, I stopped wondering.

I was moved to the regular library. Where I'd have my own office. With a desk and a chair that reclined. And AC.

Man, I was praising for days.

―――――

Angola's so large that you can go decades without seeing the same person twice. Even so, I didn't ever forget about the guy with the tomato juice. Letting go of his arm and walking away was another sign that my life was really starting to change.

Years later I saw the guy again. He was reading, like he always was, but not a crime novel. His eyes were locked on a Bible.

I said hi, and he looked up at me.

"You don't remember me, do you?" I said.

It took a moment, but then his face broke into the widest smile.

"Oh, man!" he said. "You could have broken my arm that day, but you didn't. And that changed my life. You held back, and I knew it was something to do with God. I've been seeking him ever since. I'm born-again."

A part of me was stunned and couldn't believe it. But another part just smiled. Wasn't it just like God to use that incident to spark change in both our lives?

I learned a new mantra that day: Don't ever tell me what God can't do!

———

The more I saw God at work refining my character, the more desperate I was for change in one specific area of my life. I'd been feeling it for years, ever since the trial. Ever since I'd sat in the courtroom and looked over at the victim's mother. Years later, much of the trial faded from my memory—I remembered the judge's kind voice, the DA's aggression, and my own lawyer's apathy—but the mother's face was seared in my brain. The image of her crying had never left me. I'd never seen anyone so overwhelmed by sorrow. Never seen anyone so tortured by pain. Never thought I could wound someone so greatly.

Early on in Angola, I had started praying for her regularly—and by the time I was starting to see my spiritual life take root, I was praying for her longer and more often than anyone else. But even that didn't feel like enough. Prayer was good and important, but I wanted it to lead to real change as well. I just didn't have a clue what.

The breakthrough came one day in the Christian library. I was with a group of others watching a video about forgiveness and reconciliation when it hit me. What I wanted more than anything—even more than my freedom from Angola—was the chance to have a conversation with the victim's mother and ask her for forgiveness.

From then on, my prayers had focus—to find a way to contact the victim's mother. It was illegal for me to contact anyone in the victim's family directly, either myself or through another individual. The only way would be through an organization like a church. Attempting it on my own could earn me at the very minimum a long spell in the dungeon. So I prayed for the opportunity to arise, knowing only God could really make it happen.

Eric was the first person I told about it, and he encouraged me to keep the faith and keep on praying.

The second was a minister from New Orleans whom I once heard preaching.

"So," he said to me when the service was over, "when are you going home, son?"

"I don't know. But that's not the most important thing for me."

"It isn't?"

"No. I got a bigger desire than going home."

He looked confused, like he was trying to figure out whether he needed to treat me with more skepticism.

"I want to meet the mother of the boy I killed," I said. "I want to have a conversation with her. And I want to ask her to forgive me."

I don't know what I was expecting from him, but it wasn't for him to say, "Oh, okay. Well, I can help you with that."

"Really?"

"Sure."

"You know about—"

"The restrictions? Yeah. Tell me her name and where she's from, and I'll have my church office reach out to her."

Which is exactly what he did.

A month later, he was back. He'd found the newspaper report about the trial. He'd made contact with her other son, who had given him her number.

"I told her you really want to meet her."

"What did she say?"

"At first she said yes. But then she changed her mind. She says she's not ready right now. I'm sorry, Ronnie."

I'd been quietly praying for her for years. I'd never wanted anything as desperately as I'd wanted to meet with her. But hearing this news didn't crush me or leave me disappointed. I felt the opposite. I felt encouraged, like I had just received confirmation that I was on the right path. Our meeting would happen; I was sure of it. All I could do was pray even harder. Everything else I would have to leave to God.

28 | BIBLE COLLEGE

I wasn't the only one experiencing a profound transformation in those days. Angola itself was changing, as more and more inmates found hope and purpose in their faith. We were embers blown back into life, and a fire was starting to light up so much of Angola's darkness.

A lot of it came down to the vision of one man: Warden Burl Cain. He had taken up his post in 1995, two summers after I had arrived in the prison. Warden Cain was a man of faith, a man of vision, and a man of action. He hadn't wasted any time unleashing all three on Angola. The number of clubs, programs, and churches that were accessible to prisoners grew rapidly, but that was just the start.

Not long after he arrived, it was announced that a Bible college would be established. I'd never heard of such a thing inside a prison, but as more information came out, the more people talked about it. It was to be run by the New Orleans Baptist Theological Seminary, and the teaching staff would come into Angola to take the inmate students through four or six years of study. By the end, students would earn a bona fide associate's and then bachelor's degree. The program would offer a full range of classes in everything from Greek to hermeneutics, the same classes the seminary students could access on the outside. Best of all, those enrolled in the Bible college wouldn't have to work elsewhere in the prison, *and* they would be paid twenty cents an hour to put toward books and study materials.

The program was popular right from the start, but not with me. The Bible college started in 1995, and at that point, the embers of my faith were barely warm, especially to me. I was in survival mode back then. But after Bishop Tannehill got me into church, and after Tony Roberts started encouraging me to trust God for my future, the idea of enrolling became more and more appealing. So when I got sent to Camp D, Bible college was the ideal way out.

Everyone who served in the Camp D church like I did wanted to apply. Enrollment was limited, so I took extra care with my application. A little too much care, in fact, as I was so slow that I missed the submission deadline. Everyone else who applied from Camp D—including Steve and Z-Man—was successful. What stung even more was the fact that as soon as they started classes and disappeared for most of the day, I was one of the only members of the church leadership team left out. I felt like I'd been sent into spiritual isolation.

———

Camp D was violent. Camp D was isolated. Camp D was the last place I wanted to be in Angola. And yet, Camp D turned out to be exactly what I needed. With almost everyone else heading off to the Main Prison each day to attend their classes, I had to step up. I facilitated some small groups and joined new teams. I spent a lot of time with the pastor—a wonderful man named Pastor Joe—and did a lot of growing up.

Yes, I stopped cussing and learned to put aside my instinct to retaliate if someone laid a finger on me. But even more, I learned about what Pastor Joe called "the ministry of presence."

He was full of wisdom.

"It's far better to have a listening ear than a talking mouth," he'd say often.

"Most people are not healed by the laying on of hands. They're healed by listening ears."

"When you're sitting with someone, listen. Then listen some more. And when you're done listening, listen again."

"You may think you have the answer to someone's question, but it's better to help them find that answer for themselves than to give it to them direct."

I had so many opportunities to put his wisdom to the test, like when a prisoner's son had died. It was always down to one of the pastors to pass on the death message, and on this particular day, I was the only one around. Once I gave the inmate the news, I had the strongest sense that what I needed to do was stay there and do nothing more than listen.

Hours passed.

I sat silent when he did. I cried when he cried. I laughed when he laughed as he told his favorite stories from his boy's childhood.

From the middle of the night right through to the moment when the first light of dawn came through the windows, we just sat together in his dorm. I did nothing more than listen, and it was enough.

Pastor Joe taught me that it's difficult to be a successful hypocrite in prison. You can't talk to people about love and forgiveness in a church meeting and then treat people badly in your dorm after. In fact, when you're in prison, most conversations about faith don't take place in church at all. They happen when you're in the shower, on the toilet, or just trying to get some sleep after a long day. You can't hide your failings, and you can't pretend to be something you're not. There's no better place in the world to learn how to be a pastor.

———

As I was learning to pastor others, something great happened in Camp D that healed one of my deepest wounds. Even though I was talking to my dad every Saturday on the phone, he'd still not visited me. It had been a decade since my arrest, a decade since I'd been able to hug him and feel his strong arms pulling me close. I'd learned to accept it and tried not to force my dad to change his mind, but the pain was always raw, always real.

But then, without much warning, it happened.

I was talking to my stepmom, Lil Mama, one day when she said they were coming to see me.

"Who? You and Penny?"

"That's right, me and your sister. And your daddy too."

I was in shock.

Two weeks later I was still stunned to walk into the visiting shed and see him sitting there—one of the only dads I'd ever seen visit their sons in prison. We talked awhile, cried a lot, and mostly I just let those strong arms remind me that no matter what I'd done, I was still his son, still his boy whom he loved.

———

After I regained contact with my father, God had another surprise for me in Camp D. A new chaplain started working at the prison, and some of her time was allocated to supporting the work in our camp. Her name was Chaplain Bernadine St. Cyr, and as a middle-aged Black woman, she had lived through the civil rights movement. She was smart, stubborn, and wonderfully loving, and she didn't look on us as inmates but as men. Men who deserved to be treated with dignity. And I was appointed her clerk.

Every morning, before she'd arrive, I'd get her coffee ready. I wanted to look after her, and I loved to receive a smile, a nod, or a cheery "Good morning, Mr. Ronald" when she came through the door.

I was an adult who was expecting to live the rest of my life in prison, yet God was giving me opportunities to still feel like a child again.

That's powerful medicine.

I'd been in Camp D for almost three summers when the opportunity to apply to Bible college came round again. This time I made sure my application wasn't late.

I started with two classes, one on the book of Acts and another designed to teach us to study the New Testament in its original Greek. I was just fine with the first class, but the Greek left me confused and frustrated. I'd never learned a foreign language before, and my brain just didn't seem capable of taking on one that came with a whole new alphabet. I was on the verge of quitting when I was invited to join a class that one of my pastors was running. He made the subject accessible and simple, and soon I was loving studying again.

Understanding even just a little Greek shed new light on Scripture and allowed me to approach new classes with confidence and curiosity. When I started studying hermeneutics, I was intrigued to learn how much of my Western culture I needed to put aside if I was going to understand the ancient Middle Eastern culture in which the Bible was first written. The more I understood about context, the more the Bible came alive to me. I learned to go beneath the surface and appreciate the Old Testament for more than the macho stuff featuring warriors and death and battle. I learned about the New Testament, about dispensation, about grace.

When I'd been given permission to first move into General Population, the officer had given me some advice: "Out there in GP it's not *penitentiary*. It's *pay attention*." He'd meant it as a warning, reminding me not to trust anybody, and I had followed the advice carefully. But the more I grew spiritually, the more I understood another way of interpreting his words: In Angola, God was at work in all kinds of places. It was up to me to pay attention and see what he was doing and how I might join in.

PART 5

GOD KNOWS WHERE YOU ARE

29 | THE PROPHECY

I was thirty years old when I stood with my family beside me, a cap on my head and gown on my shoulders as we posed for photos. It was 2005, and I had just graduated from Bible college with a bachelor's degree in theology. Just like any other graduate, for me the ceremony marked not only the end of years of challenging work but the arrival of new opportunities. If I wanted, I could apply to become a missionary within the Louisiana prison system. It would mean serving two years of my sentence in another prison, working alongside the chaplaincy department as a pastor. It was a ticket out of Angola, if only for a couple of summers.

On paper, the prospect of leaving Angola and relocating was appealing. Angola was still the most notorious prison in the state, with thousands of inmates convicted of the most serious crimes. But having been there twelve summers, it was now familiar to me. I had friends in Angola, and I no longer had to prove myself to anyone. In a strange way, Angola felt like home.

Yet I knew God was calling me to be a missionary. I knew he was going to send me out somewhere to be used by him. I had known it for years, ever since I first heard the prophecy.

The prophecy was a few typed paragraphs on a piece of paper. I don't remember how anyone in Angola first got hold of it, but I do remember that the note started circulating around the churches in the prison sometime back in 1998. I was just seeing the first signs of spiritual transformation in my life, and I was hungry for any sign that God was on the move. When I first encountered this single piece of paper with the words *Bill Yount, 1994* typed at the bottom, I was instantly fascinated.

Bill described how one night God woke him up around midnight. He thought it was late, then he realized it wasn't late for God because God doesn't sleep.

God had a question for Bill.

Where do people keep their most prized possessions?

They keep them in the bank, in the safe, thought Bill. *They lock them away.*

Likewise, said God, *that's where my most prized possessions are. They're all locked up. They're in the prisons.*

Then Bill saw a massive number of prisoners, some with gold auras, some with bronze, all of them walking over the prison walls. They moved out into communities, changing them with the gospel. All the places where the big-name churches hadn't done their job, the prisoners were going there. The prisoners were becoming the pastors.

I loved every word of it. I must have read that prophecy a hundred times a year. I shared it with everyone I could: people who believed and those who didn't. I read it in church services that I was leading and sent it to other churches within the prison so others could hear it too. I even got the prison DJ to read it on-air. As far as I was concerned, Bill Yount's prophecy was fact. It was going to happen, and somehow, I was going to see it with my own eyes.

The Bible college was proof. It had grown dramatically since it began, and I wasn't the only one who was convinced it was somehow linked to the prophecy. By the time I graduated, well over one hundred graduates were leaving the Bible college each year, joining all the other previous graduates who were still in Angola. These graduates went back to their churches like trained mechanics working on a car. They didn't just have the instinct and the training to diagnose the problems; they had the tools required to fix them.

So when I graduated Bible college and let my thoughts turn to the prospect of my becoming a missionary, here's how my mind went.

If one day I'm going to be a part of Bill Yount's prophecy, then I need to be ready.

If I want to be ready, then I need to be ready for anything. I can't be putting limits on where I will and won't let God send me.

If I'm not going to have limits, I've got to be ready to go somewhere uncomfortable.

Once I'd decided that, the rest was easy. All I needed to do was wait, pray, and see who God would send as a messenger to reveal where he wanted me to go.

———

I'd never had any direct contact with Warden Cain before, but I knew who he was. Everyone in Angola did. I'd seen him walking around a few times. He was short, barrel-chested, with snow-white hair and a thick Louisiana drawl that made him impossible to miss. Within the boundaries of the Louisiana State Penitentiary, he *was* the law. He was more powerful than the president of the United States and didn't have to answer to anyone. But he never hid his faith, and we all knew he took his God-given calling seriously.

When I heard he had a message for me, I was nervous. I didn't suspect that he was somehow caught up in whatever God was planning, but when I heard what he wanted to ask me—would I be willing to go and serve as a missionary in Camp J?—I knew I'd received my God-given orders.

Camp J was the worst place possible. The prison within the prison. It might not have had Camp D's reputation for violence, but it more than made up for it with the conditions and the inmates. Most of them had been sent there because they were considered dangerous to others, though a few were high-profile inmates who would have been targets in General Population. Among them were a few big-name rappers, including New Orleans's very own C-Murder. But status outside of Angola meant nothing in Camp J, and C-Murder was locked in his single cell twenty-three hours a day just like all the others.

It was the most depressing camp in Angola, and a lot of the inmates were struggling with their mental health. They were held in their cells like animals in pens. They were angry. They were scared. They turned to suicide at an alarming rate. It was the worst of the worst.

There was a small dormitory in Camp J for inmates who worked as cooks, orderlies, and other essential roles, but because of the isolated nature of Camp J, they had practically zero access to any facilities or clubs. Nobody in their right mind would ever volunteer to go there. Nobody in their right mind would ever choose somewhere so uncomfortable.

Apart from me.

30 | THE VISIT

Camp J was even worse than I anticipated. With four hundred angry, scared men locked away like that, the walls themselves felt like they were sweating despair. It didn't take long for me to understand the scope of my mission. I was there to serve, to treat inmates well, and to say yes to whatever opportunity God put in my way. That was all. That was enough.

At some point, maybe a few months in, I could feel the pressure. The sense of despair was highly infectious, and I started to feel isolated in Camp J. I felt like I was locked away with the security risks, removed from the opportunities that inmates in other camps had access to. Bit by bit, I found myself feeding on a new worry: I had said yes to God, but what if he had forgotten about me in Camp J?

One part of my week became even more of a lifeline than it had been before: church. I wasn't able to access anywhere near the same number of church callouts I had previously, but those that I could sign up for, I did. In addition to Sunday services, I was facilitating a group called *Experiencing God* that met back at the Main Prison. We'd look at the Bible and the *Experiencing God* workbook and give space for the guys to focus on the subject at hand. I'd facilitated a few group studies before, and I always enjoyed seeing the way God caught people's attention.

He got my attention in a major way when I ran the course in Camp J.

We were at the end of a session where we'd been talking about the ways God can use different people, and I asked the same questions I always did.

"What jumped out at you? What really spoke to you?"

One guy leaned forward in his chair—his eyes half-closed like he'd just woken up and was trying to hold on to a dream.

"God knows where you are," he said as the room listened in silence. "And he can cause anybody at any time to know where you are too. That's what I noticed."

It was just what I needed to hear. I'd been feeling isolated and locked away, and I'd let myself start to get a little sidetracked with the fear that I might just be permanently forgotten. I needed to be reminded of the truth about God: He never lets us go. He never turns his back. None of us are hidden from his love.

———

"That's him. That's Ronnie."

It was the very next day after the *Experiencing God* session, and I was back in Camp J, getting ready to do my rounds visiting the inmates. I was a little lost in my thoughts and hadn't noticed anyone approaching until I heard them.

I looked up to see who was talking about me. A couple of guys—visitors with a video camera—were being escorted over in my direction. They had the wide-eyed look of guys who hadn't spent any time behind bars.

"Ronald Olivier? We're from Brooklyn Tabernacle Church, and we're making a short film about what God is doing here in Angola. Pastor Gary Norris told us we had to come find you. Said we had to interview you. You got time to talk?"

I had nothing to say, but only because I was so shocked. It had been less than twenty-four hours since I'd been reminded that God knew where I was—and that he could send whomever he wanted to find me at any time he wanted. These two visitors looking for me by name was all the proof I needed.

It took me a few moments to recover myself and agree to their request. I spent a little while with them that day, telling my story. I talked about what it was like growing up where I did, how I never had any peace and was convinced that if I hadn't ended up in Angola, I'd surely be dead by now. I spoke about meeting Jesus in the holding cell while twelve people decided whether I got to live or die. I spoke about how I was now experiencing the peace that surpasses understanding, the kind that makes you comfortable in the most uncomfortable of situations.

I didn't have any time to prepare what I said. I was just talking from the heart, saying whatever I knew to be true.

"I wouldn't trade it for anything," I said. "It's like it says in Ecclesiastes 7:8: 'Better is the end of a thing than the beginning thereof.' Angola is not the end for me."

When we finished and the guys from Brooklyn Tab had said goodbye, I took some time to think about it all. The thinking lasted for days. Even weeks.

I was stunned that God would move so quickly to confirm what I'd heard in the *Experiencing God* group. I never doubted *whether* he could move that quickly, but the fact that he had *chosen* to do so blew me away.

Then there was the film itself. The guys had told me about their lead pastor, Jim Cymbala. They told me about his passion to see God break through and bring real change to real lives. The more they told me about what Pastor Cymbala was doing at Brooklyn Tab, the more I thought about Bill Yount's prophecy. Maybe, in some weird way, the two were connected.

I had a hunch that God was up to something, that he was going to use the film to introduce me to people who might wind up being significant in my life. And while I knew all of this was about the goodness and grace of God and not about my own efforts or hard work, I couldn't help thinking that none of this would have happened if I'd not said yes to Camp J. If I'd stayed where I was relatively comfortable, in the place where I was not so dependent on God, maybe I'd have missed out on this lesson from him. It made me want to make a solemn vow: that from then on, I would always try to be bold in my faith. No matter what sacrifice was required, I would go against the grain of comfort. After all, God is not nearly as concerned about us being comfortable as he is about us being conformed into the image of Christ Jesus.

Months later, I was still thinking about the film. But now, I wasn't wondering about the possibility of it being used by God. I was marveling at what he had already done through it. The film had been translated into other languages, and there were reports of people in the underground churches in China getting hold of it. A part of me simply could not believe it, but it was proof again of the timeless truth: *Don't tell me what God can't do!*

31 | A MISSIONARY'S CALLING

If you're over thirty-five years old in Angola, have served at least twenty years of your sentence, and have not had a single write-up in at least two years, you can become a Trusty. This special category of prisoner gets all kinds of privileges, from taking on certain jobs that use dangerous equipment—such as cooks, gardeners, or electricians—to even being allowed outside the prison gates without direct supervision. Trusties can live in their own camp within the prison, where there are fewer rules and the TV's never turned off. If they're on a callout or are visiting someone in the hospital wing, Trusties don't have to wait for their scheduled ride to take them from camp to camp. Instead, they can flag down any passing state vehicle that's driving around Angola. They can even ride in the front. If you're going to spend the rest of your life locked up, being a Trusty will make those decades just a little less painful.

Soon after I arrived in Camp J, Assistant Warden Sam Smith suggested I put my name in for Trusty. I was okay on the lack of write-ups, but I was very short of the twenty-years-served threshold. I wasn't thirty-five either. The warden told me to apply anyway. I thought about it for a while and eventually put in to be a Class B Trusty. Class B had most of the same benefits as Class A, but I wouldn't be allowed out the main gates without supervision. I didn't mind at all about that, and I figured I wasn't likely to get it anyway.

The letter came back quickly. I'd been made a Class A Trusty.

Between this, the Brooklyn Tab film, and the time I was enjoying as an inmate minister, I was feeling good. I knew God was with me, that he was looking out for me, that I could handle anything ahead of me with his help.

I also knew that none of this meant I should sit back, congratulate myself on doing well, and take it easy. Instead of seeing God's favor as some kind of reward, I saw it for what it really was: an equipping, a season of preparation for something yet to come.

———

Nothing could have prepared me for what happened one day at a picnic visit the church had organized. Dawn was there with the girls, along with Mama and other members of my family, and we'd spent the first part of the visit standing in a big old circle made up of at least twenty inmates and their families. We prayed. It was a special time, one of those rare moments when the prison gates fade just a little into the background.

After we'd prayed, it was time for the barbecue. The air was turning smoky, and I was getting ready to load up my plate, when Dawn got down onto one knee in front of me.

"Will you marry me?"

I was in shock. Real shock. I knew what my answer was instantly, but there was no way I could say it. Not there, not in front of everyone. I didn't want to reject her and embarrass her like that, and a part of me loved her. She had been loyal to me—visiting so often and encouraging the girls to see me as their dad. I guess I felt obligated to her for all that. So I looked her in the eye and said, "Yes. I'll marry you, Dawn."

I didn't feel great about it. But the way I saw it, between Dawn's chaotic life and my being in prison, this wedding was never going to happen anyway.

Turned out I was wrong.

Six months later we'd passed all the checks the prison put in place, sat through a couple of interviews, and even got permission direct from Warden Cain himself. It was really happening. My head was spinning. I could have gotten out of it, I guess, but the sense of obligation had grown. I felt like I owed her. Plus, part of me wanted it as well. It's a powerful thing to have someone love you like that when you're doing a life sentence and despite the great possibility you will never be free.

On our wedding day, we were allowed ten guests. The ceremony was in the chapel, and the reception was in the visiting shed. The shed looked real nice, and we had a cake and a bit of music for dancing. Some of my friends even fixed it so Dawn and I could have some time together on our own. It wasn't part of the official Angola policy, and I spent the hour we had together fearing that someone was going to come busting through the door at any point and give me a write-up. With all that pressure, things didn't quite work out as planned.

———

On February 12, 2007, the next real spiritual challenge finally came. I had been inside Angola for thirteen summers when I knew it was time for me to go and be a missionary in a prison elsewhere. I got assigned to Avoyelles Correctional Center in Cottonport, Louisiana, and was given the task of helping with the pastoral team that ran the church.

I was nervous the day I left Angola. It was my first time out the front gates since I'd arrived in the summer of 1993. Despite the violence, the high levels of suicide, and the threat of danger I was leaving behind me, I was anxious about what lay ahead. Strangely, there was one area in which Angola had a better reputation than smaller prisons in the state. Because Angola's inmates were all serving fifty years to life, Warden Cain avoided antagonizing them by enforcing petty rules. Instead of getting stressed about uniforms or whether people were walking in single-file lines, Angola let these little things go and focused on the major issues like drugs and violence. The other prisons in the state took a different approach. They came down hard on anyone breaking even the most minor rules. Moving to Avoyelles would be hard enough for me in terms of establishing myself among the inmates, but now I'd have to deal with uptight, rule-keeping guards as well.

———

I stepped off the bus at Avoyelles, handcuffed and shackled. They had dogs barking outside, and I was taken straight in for a full search. If they wanted to make a strong first impression, it worked.

I was just about finished when the chaplain who had interviewed me for the post, Chaplain White, showed up. He told me to come see him in the chapel as soon as I'd taken my possessions to the dorm.

Old habits die hard, and I could feel myself tensing up as I entered the forty-bed dorm. The other inmates were out at the time, so I loaded my things into my locker and figured I'd establish myself among my new roommates later on.

Chaplain White was warm and encouraging, introducing me to all the other inmate ministers as well as the pastor.

"This is a big day for Pastor Clouser," he said.

"How come?"

"He's getting discharged tonight. Fifteen years later, and it's all about to end."

I told the guy congratulations and found a seat. A church service was about to begin, and the space was filling up. I really felt like I could do with some worship, some prayer, and an encouraging word from whoever was preaching.

"You come on up here, Olivier," said Chaplain White, pointing to an empty chair behind the pulpit on the stage. It wasn't my preferred choice.

The service began with Chaplain White talking about Pastor

Clouser's departure and how great it was to be able to share this moment with him. I'd always liked seeing guys leave prison, but this time it all got weird real fast.

"So," Chaplain White said as soon as Pastor Clouser sat down, "it's time for me to announce your new pastor here at Grace Fellowship."

I looked around me. I'd been introduced to at least ten inmate ministers, and I wondered which one it was going to be.

"Come on up here, Ronald Olivier."

I looked back at Chaplain White. For a moment I wondered if he was making a joke, but between his smile and the frowns from the inmate ministers, I knew he was serious.

I didn't want to make a scene, so I did what he asked and said a few words of greeting from the pulpit. Then I sat back down as quickly as I could, praying that God would somehow show me how this was going to work out.

After the service, I asked Chaplain White for a few minutes alone in his office.

"Please," I said once the door was closed. "I didn't come here to be the pastor. I just came to help out with the ministry."

"I know, Pastor Ronald."

"And I've been looking at Grace Fellowship, and it seems to me you've already got a whole lot of people capable of running this thing—ushers and a choir and all those inmate ministers. You don't need an outsider coming in, and certainly not one who's only just got off the bus."

"I hear you," he said, nodding and looking like he was 100 percent genuine. "You're still the pastor."

———

As it turned out, I had no reason at all to be anxious about the inmates in Avoyelles. The guys in my dorm were just fine, and I quickly felt relaxed around them. The inmate ministers though? That was a whole other story.

Right from the start, they were hostile. Chaplain White was quick to tell me they'd had missionaries at Grace Fellowship before. Most of them had just graduated Bible college and wanted to make sure all the other inmate ministers knew it and did exactly what they were told.

"I guess it left a bitter taste in their mouths," he said.

That was a huge understatement. Those guys fought me on every little suggestion I made, from introducing new styles of worship music into the services to setting up new schedules. I'd never been a leader in that capacity before, though I was a minister on staff at the Leadership Builder program in Angola. I'd never experienced any real conflict within the churches I'd been involved with, so this was all new to me. I was desperately in need of some wisdom.

I got the wisdom I needed direct from the source. God put it on my heart that the only thing I needed to do was to show these guys love, and he gave me the resources to back it up too. The more they opposed me, the easier I found it to treat them well. I gave in to their wishes, preferred them, and told them it was fine if they didn't want to try the things I suggested. I didn't stop with the suggestions, but I made sure they knew that when it came to a choice between getting my own way and serving them, they'd win out every time.

It didn't take long before they stopped fighting and started joining in with the changes. That's when I realized one of the most powerful truths ever: nothing can stand in the way of pure, uncut agape. Selfless, Christlike love is hands down the most powerful force on the planet.

By the time I'd been at Avoyelles six months, I felt as though I'd gained a decade of pastoral experience. Six years of Bible college had trained me well for the ministry, but it took a real-life church—with hurting, awkward, everyday people—for me to know that I was finally becoming a pastor.

———

Agape love is powerful, but it's not magic. It can melt hearts, but it doesn't control them. It builds a bridge for people to cross over from pain and fear into hope and love, but it does not force them to walk. Agape invites, and the answer is either yes or no.

While the inmate ministers were softening and changing, it became clear that someone else at Grace Fellowship was digging in: Chaplain White. He was my boss, so I'd meet with him regularly and ask his permission to start various programs or make certain changes within Grace Fellowship. Every time he gave some version of the same answer: no.

"We can't do that here."

"That's not how Grace Fellowship works."

"A change like that wouldn't make anyone happy."

I don't know if it was because Chaplain White was a traditional Baptist, if we had a personality clash, or if we just had genuine differences of opinion, but I struggled with his rigid approach. At that point in my life, everything I'd learned about being a Christian I'd learned in Angola. There, church was seen as a vehicle for change in the lives of the inmates. In the very prison where movies like *Dead Man Walking* and *Monster's Ball* were set—movies that helped show the world how desperate and desolate Angola was—church was actually a powerful beacon of light and hope. God-given change was embraced there, in everything from the programs and services to the chaplains, minsters, and members.

Chaplain White's refusal to do anything but the same old, same old left me confused. I did a lot of praying in those days at Avoyelles, always laying the same question before the Lord: *What do you want me to do here?*

The answer came as one of those hunches you get sometimes, the kind where you know the first step you need to take but have absolutely no idea where you're going to end up. It was a leap of faith, I guess. Nothing more, nothing less.

"Chap," I said to him next time we met. "What about getting an intercession team going?"

He said yes, and I hid my surprise. I quickly went searching for the guys in Grace Fellowship who earnestly loved to pray, and within a week or two we had a prayer request box in the chapel and a fully formed intercession team that was ready for its first two-hour meeting early one Sunday morning.

"Look," I said before we got started, "y'all can pray for whatever's in the prayer box and whatever else you want to be praying for, but I also want you to pray for Chaplain White. I need you to be praying that God would either change him or move him."

I felt a little nervous saying it, but I knew it was the right thing to be asking.

Three weeks later, I had the confirmation.

"I got bad news for you, Pastor Ronald," said Chaplain White as I walked into his office for one of our regular meetings.

I could feel the tension spark within me. "What's up, Chap?"

"I'll be leaving in two weeks."

32 | BIG RU AND ME

Big Ru was big. Three hundred pounds big. Six-four big. The kind of big that made him perfect as an enforcer out on the streets. The kind of big that meant wherever Big Ru was, violence was never far away.

I first met Big Ru at church in Angola. He was rough around the edges, like we all were at the beginning of our journeys, but Big Ru had an appetite for God that was undeniable. He could take correction and guidance as well as any person I'd ever met, and it was a privilege to see him grow in faith.

Big Ru wrote me when I was at Avoyelles, right around the time I was struggling with Chaplain White. Big Ru explained that he'd graduated Bible college and was looking to become an inmate missionary. What did I think about him coming to join me? I told him it was a great idea.

Now, when you get to know Big Ru, you see a man who wants more of God in his life. You see someone who is open to change and who has already come a long, long way. You see his heart and his potential. But when you meet him for the first time, chances are you won't see any of that good stuff. You just see his threatening size and the beetle-eyed stare he gives you. It's hard to get past the biceps the size of tree trunks, which are folded over his chest as he stands motionless in any room, like a grizzly bear trying to figure out which prey to attack first.

Yet, for some reason I can only put down to God, Chaplain White was fine with Big Ru becoming assistant pastor at Grace Fellowship, and my old friend from Angola arrived just before the chaplain left.

Big Ru quickly settled in at Avoyelles—nobody ever dared mess with him in prison—and the two of us worked well together. Big Ru would accompany me on my rounds, going from dormitory to dormitory, checking in on the guys, and making ourselves available to talk if they wanted.

Big Ru being Big Ru, he had his own unique interpretation of the assistant pastor role. He figured that as my assistant, one of his main duties was to make sure I was always safe and that the other inmates knew they couldn't mess with me. I appreciated the concern, but it created some problems that needed addressing.

"Big Ru, when you stand at the door to the chapel like you're a bouncer on Bourbon Street, it kind of puts people off. They don't need to feel intimidated when they come to church. They need to feel welcome."

He took the advice and moved to a less visible part of the chapel when people came in.

Four months after he arrived at Avoyelles, Big Ru messed up on a whole other level. It was one of those mistakes that is hard to remember years later, partly because of the passing of time, but mainly because of what happened after. The real headline wasn't the sin; it was the redemption that followed.

Whatever Big Ru did, the short-term consequence was that I had to ask him to step down from certain parts of his assistant pastor job, including preaching in the chapel and sitting at the front by the pulpit. This hit him hard, and his reaction when I told him he would be benched for a few weeks was just what I'd hoped to avoid. He was furious with me.

I'll admit that I was more than a little intimidated by the sight and the sound of an angry Big Ru. He yelled and glared, and I could see his giant bear hands itching to break something. But after a few moments, he calmed. He agreed to step down for a while.

He could have stayed away, turning his back on me and Grace

Fellowship. I would have understood if he had—after all, isn't it always tempting to run away from pain instead of toward it? But in the weeks that followed, I watched Big Ru walk into every meeting at the chapel. He'd sit on the front row on Sundays, eyes closed in the worship, wide-open in the sermon. I'd never seen him hungrier for God.

One day he came up at the end of the service, tears and snot covering his face.

"I want to ask you something," he said, his rich bass voice cracked and broken.

"Anything, Big Ru."

"I want to ask you to forgive me."

I was silent for a while, but not because it was a difficult thing for me to do. I was just lost in the moment, thanking God for his work in my brother's life.

Big Ru must have sensed my hesitation. "This is nothin' about me getting up preaching again. It's about me just owning what I did. You can fire me if you want, get someone else to be the assistant pastor. All that matters to me is that you know I'm sorry."

The more time I spent with Big Ru, the more convinced I was of the truth of Bill Yount's prophecy. Even though it was hard for many people to see, so much gold was locked up in Big Ru. So much about him was evidence of God at work. He was an inmate other inmates wanted to avoid, but he was so clearly loved by his Maker. There was no clearer picture of God's treasure than Big Ru.

The more I thought about it, the more I understood that God was actively involved in changing lives like Big Ru's. He was unloading that agape love on him in massive, Big Ru–sized quantities. Seeing Big Ru in action like this—turning to God when he was hurt, looking for forgiveness—made it obvious that God wasn't just keeping his most treasured possessions locked away in cold storage. He was using them, refining them, honing them, and getting them ready for whatever he had planned for further down the line.

33 | DR. DRAPER GETS US OUT

When I first met Dr. Leslie Draper—a former marine turned church pastor who replaced Chaplain White in Avoyelles—I had no idea of the extent to which he would affect my life. That state of ignorance didn't last long. It took about a month for me to figure out that though he was half the size of Big Ru, when Dr. Draper was on a mission from God, there was no wall he couldn't smash through.

"I want to take you to church," he said one day to Big Ru and me.

"Here? To Grace Fellowship?"

"No, to my home church in Simmesport. I'm thinking this Sunday would be good. There's a special service on, with a banquet after. If you're happy to come, I'll go talk to the warden."

Neither of us said anything other than yes, but the whole thing sounded impossible. Only Trusties were allowed out for something like this, but our Trusty status had not transferred with us from Angola. At Avoyelles, you needed fewer than seven years left on your sentence before you could apply. Since Big Ru and I were both lifers, we assumed the warden would not allow it.

"Warden said yes," Dr. Draper told us the next day.

"Really?" I asked.

Dr. Draper gave me a look. "Really. Warden said I must have lost my mind, but he couldn't think of a good enough reason to say no. So, Sunday it is. Security will drive you over about nine thirty."

Sunday came, and Big Ru and I were standing in front of the security guys, ready to go. There were two of them—an older, heavy white guy and a young Black guy. From the look of the older guy, he'd been in Avoyelles for decades, and there was nothing he hadn't seen. Nothing, that is, until nine thirty on this particular Sunday.

In his hand was a clipboard that held the trip instructions. He was staring at the paper, frowning. The first signs of sweat started to show on his brow.

"Can't be right . . ." he muttered. "Must be a mistake."

"What's wrong?" asked the young guy.

"It says here 'no restraints.' That can't be right. These two are lifers."

They both stared at the paper, then looked back up to the pair of us. They both took extra time staring at Big Ru.

"I'll call the supervisor," said the older guy, heading off toward a nearby office.

We could hear him clearly from within. "Really? You're sure about that?"

More than a hint of sweat now shimmered on his brow when he returned. He was flushed pink, glancing nervously between Big Ru, me, and his colleague.

Big Ru and I sat—unshackled and smiling—on either side of the young guy in the back of the patrol car. He was armed, like the driver, and if we'd wanted to, it would have been easy for Big Ru and me to take a gun and make our escape. I knew the old guy was keeping a close check on the two of us in his rearview mirror, but escaping was the last thing on my mind. It was the first time either Big Ru or I had been out of prison without being cuffed and shackled, and I wanted to savor every moment of it.

After about an hour and a half on the road, we pulled up outside

the Tree of Calvary Baptist Church. Walking across the grass toward
the open door, I didn't have the words to begin to describe my feelings.
I reached down and dug my hand into the free earth, driving grass
and dirt under my fingernails. After almost fifteen years in jail, the
very air seemed different in the free world. It was clearer out here. It
made my head spin.

Dr. Draper welcomed us inside and showed us to our seats. He
sat us on the stage, beside the pulpit, while the two security officers
moved off toward the back. Big Ru and I sat in silence, soaking in
the sounds of the church filling up. As soon as the service began,
Dr. Draper introduced us, welcomed us, and explained that since this
was a special service celebrating his anniversary as pastor, he was especially pleased that we could be there to share it with him. I'd been
in plenty of church services back in Angola where family members
were invited, but this was different. In Angola the visitors were invited
into our world, but here in Simmesport, we were invited into theirs.
I felt like I belonged among the good people of the Tree of Calvary
Baptist Church, but I also knew it was only temporary. If I had any
doubts about that, the two armed men at the back reminded me.
Their jobs depended on us—on Big Ru and me being delivered back
to the Avoyelles Correctional Center later that afternoon.

I was a little dazed by it all. But gradually, the service washed over
me like a summer breeze, and I could feel myself settle. The sound of
so many people behind me singing, the noise of all those voices praying, the silence that followed—they all filled me with awe.

It was after the service, when Dr. Draper invited everyone to stay
for the anniversary banquet, that something changed. Over plates
piled high, Big Ru and I sat and talked with the people Dr. Draper
wanted us to meet. We filled our mouths with fried chicken and
gumbo as we listened to people share their stories and talk about their
pastor, Dr. Draper. He was the third generation of Draper men to
serve the town of Simmesport—a former plantation that Dr. Draper's

grandfather used to work on before eventually becoming mayor. We devoured piles of macaroni and laughed with them as they joked. I could feel the goodness of God from my head all the way down to my belly.

When we'd eaten all we could, there were still pies, cakes, and all kinds of desserts to enjoy. I closed my eyes and let the flavors of the food and the warmth of good conversation float deep within me. I was caught up in the ministry of fellowship, and it was a beautiful, beautiful experience.

34 | LIFE IN ABUNDANCE

All the time I was in Avoyelles, I tried to keep in contact with people. Mama would visit when she could, and even my dad and Lil Mama were making the long drive from Jacksonville to see me when they could. Dawn backed off a little, but it didn't worry me. The last thing I wanted was for her to feel like she was trapped with me. I was the one who had been given a life sentence, not her.

I kept in contact with my old friend Eric, making regular phone calls back to him in Angola. We kept each other updated on what was going on in our lives, and I often found myself talking about the things Dr. Draper was teaching me about leadership and the challenges of being a pastor.

One day when Eric and I spoke, I was telling him about an inmate I'd had contact with recently. In the space of a few weeks, he'd lost both his adult children in two separate incidents. Both times I'd taken the death message to him, and on each occasion, I'd asked if he wanted me to stay with him awhile. I sat next to him on his bed, hardly saying anything but practicing what Dr. Draper called "the ministry of presence"—just like Pastor Joe had when I was back in Camp D. I sat with the man, listening and praying. It was all I could do.

"If you ask me," Eric said after I was done talking, "it sounds like you're exactly where God wants you to be."

"I think you're right. I believe with all my heart that I'm going home one day, but I don't want to wait until I'm released to start living. Just because I'm locked doesn't mean I can't experience life in all its abundance."

35 | THE ANGOLA POLYGRAPH

Two summers after I arrived, my time serving as a missionary in Avoyelles was over. I said goodbye to my friends there, thanked Dr. Draper for all he'd done for me, and returned to Angola. I was back in the Main Prison, ready to throw myself into whatever challenge God had in store for me next.

It was good to be able to catch up with old friends. Eric was doing well, as were plenty of others I'd gotten to know over the years. I ended up in a dorm with Pastor Norris, the inmate minister who had encouraged the two guys making the film for Brooklyn Tab to come and find me when I was working in Camp J. He was a good friend, and I was pleased to see him looking happy. Life appeared to be going well for him, though when we got to talking about our families and the fact that Christmas was just around the corner, he looked a little down.

We were eating together in the Main Prison's church office when he said, "What I want this year is to be able to buy my little daughter a real nice Christmas present. Just once, I want her to feel like there's something special in her life."

"I hear you, Pastor."

Pastor Norris leaned back in his chair and swung his feet up onto the table.

I let out a long, low whistle. He was wearing a fine pair of like-new, just-out-of-the-box G-Nikes. They were black and gold, New Orleans Saints colors. I liked them a lot, and I knew from previous trades he and I had done that they were just my size. "Okay," I said. "How about I buy those from you? What do you want for them?"

He thought for a moment. "How about $110?"

"No problem," I said. "No problem at all. You want me to get you things from the canteen?"

He shrugged. Instead, we agreed that I'd get someone in my family to send the money to someone in his, and we went about our days.

————

All the time I'd been in Avoyelles, I'd barely seen Dawn. She'd told me the four-hour drive was just too much for her, so she only visited occasionally. I'd had my suspicions that she wasn't telling me the whole story, and eventually she told me she'd been involved with another guy. I'd felt crushed by the news, but I decided to forgive her. She was my wife and had stood by me throughout everything. I knew she was under pressure, and I knew the ache of loneliness. But I couldn't stand the thought of it happening again, so I told her that while my forgiveness was genuine, if she cheated on me again, it was over.

Dawn's love language was always touch. Before I'd gone to Avoyelles, whenever she visited me in the Angola visiting shed, she would always sit close by me, holding my hand or hugging me. Now that I was back and she had only a two-hour drive to reach me, we held hands a little on our first visit, but it seemed to me that something had changed.

I didn't want to get into it right then, so we mainly talked about how the girls were getting on and things like that. I passed on the details that Pastor Norris had given me and asked her to send the money for the sneakers over. She said she was happy to do it, and the visit ended.

I was thinking about Dawn a lot in the days that followed, but when the news broke that Pastor Norris had been having a relationship with a female security officer in Angola, all thoughts of Dawn moved to the back of my mind.

I was not surprised that an inmate would have a relationship with a female security officer. More female guards worked in Angola than male guards, and I'd heard of several cases of officer-inmate romances sparking up throughout my time there. What *did* surprise me was that Pastor Norris was involved. As a Trusty, he had a lot more to lose than other inmates. And I'd assumed that as a Christian brother, he was doing everything he could to resist that particular temptation, just as I was. But what really shocked me was that the officer in question was the same person he'd asked me to send the money to. Though buying a pair of shoes from another inmate was perfectly legal in Angola, I couldn't shake the feeling that somehow this was going to come back and bite me.

Two weeks later, Pastor Norris was taken from the Main Prison and put in a dungeon cell in Camp J. Soon I got a message saying I was to attend an interview in Investigation Services—Angola's very own version of the FBI.

I'd never been in their building before, and I had no idea what to expect. I certainly wasn't expecting to see Warden Cain sitting behind a desk, staring at me as I walked in. I'd never really spoken with him at length before, and I was nervous.

"Sit down," he said, "and listen to me. I've been through your record. I know you're a good guy. You've been doing some real good things with your life in here, so all I need from you right now is the truth. You hear me?"

"Okay," I said, trying not to look around at the other security officers. Out of the corner of my eye I could see they were staring daggers at me. "Sure, Warden Cain. No problem."

"Okay, well that's good. So, where's the cell phone SIM?"

I didn't catch what he said, so I asked him to say it again.

"The cell phone SIM. Where is it?"

It was early 2011, and I'd never even heard of a SIM, let alone seen one or knew what it did. I think I'd seen a cell phone once or twice when I was out with Dr. Draper in Simmesport, but I'd never touched one. "I'm sorry, Warden Cain. I don't even know what a SIM is."

He sat back and frowned. I risked a glance at the other guys in the room. They were all frowning too.

"Okay, let me explain what's happened here for you," said Warden Cain eventually. He went on to tell me all about Pastor Norris and the security officer, and how Norris's daughter was living with the officer. During the investigation, they'd searched the library where Pastor Norris was working. In his office they'd discovered two cell phones, as well as letters addressed to him from the security officer.

"And one of those letters mentions you," said Warden Cain. "Do you want to know what it says?"

I could feel the room starting to spin.

"It says: 'I ain't got the money from Ronnie Olivier's wife yet.'"

My mouth was dry when I spoke next. "Warden Cain, all I know about Pastor Norris is that I bought some shoes from him. He wanted me to have someone in my family send the money to someone in his family, so I just passed the details he gave me to my wife. That's all that happened. I don't know anything about a cell phone, and I don't know anything about him being in no relationship with anyone."

"And that's the truth?"

"Yes, sir, Warden Cain. That's the truth."

He paused for a moment, eyes locked on mine. "Well, let's just make sure of that, shall we? We'll hook you up to a polygraph—run this all by the lie detector."

I told him it was fine by me.

"But remember this," he added as someone at the back of the room pulled a case out of a cupboard and started setting up the machine. "If you fail this test, I will crush you."

I opened my mouth to say something, but no words came. I decided to let this machine speak.

————

It took a few minutes to get the polygraph ready and all the wires attached to me correctly. I'd never taken a lie detector test before, and I was surprised how nervous I was. Warden Cain had everyone leave the room, so it was just me and one of the officers from Investigation Services making the final adjustments to the machine. My heart rate started to pick up.

"Is your name Ronald Olivier?"

"Yes."

"Is today's date March 17, 2011?"

"Yes."

After a few more basic questions, the subject turned to cell phones. I confirmed that I'd never seen one, never even used one, and had no knowledge whatsoever of anything to do with Pastor Norris and the security officer smuggling cell phones into prison.

The test was over quickly, and I sat back and breathed. The questions had been easier than I'd feared, and telling the truth had been simple.

When all the wires were off me, the guy left for a while before coming back with Warden Cain. The warden held a printout from the polygraph. His eyes were cold as he looked at me and delivered his verdict.

"You failed."

36 | LOCKED UP IN THE DUNGEON

Warden Cain ordered that I be taken straight to Camp J. I was placed in a cell I recognized from the time I worked in the camp as an inmate minister. It was the suicide watch cell, complete with a surveillance camera and close to the security office.

As soon as I was locked in, I started cleaning the cell. I needed the distraction, but I also wanted to be sure there was nothing within the cell that they could pin on me. I checked the steel frame of the bed, the back of the sink, and even the walls for loose bricks. I was looking for shanks, handcuff shims, cigarettes, and anything else that might have been hidden there. The last thing I wanted was for them to have reason to hold me any longer than necessary.

I prayed as I cleaned, but the spiritual condition of the cell wasn't as easy to deal with as the physical. Evil seemed to fill the air, and when I lay down later that night, there were moments when the oppression was so heavy, I felt like I was being pinned to the bed.

———

The next day I was moved into a new cell. I ran through the same routine there, cleaning and checking, praying all the while. But in this new cell, the sense of evil was even stronger—ten or twenty times worse. For the first time in my life, I was being attacked by the darkest thoughts imaginable.

You're never getting out of here.

You might as well kill yourself.

I'd spent long enough working in Camp J to know that suicide was a regular occurrence among the inmates there—yet I'd never thought too hard about what drove them to it. Now I felt like I knew. I felt like I was standing on a cliff's edge. One move and I could tumble over.

I heard a voice from an inmate a few cells along and recognized it instantly. I was grateful for the distraction and the chance to think about something other than the sickening pull of death.

"Pastor Norris? Is that you? It's Ronnie. Over here."

"Ronnie, for real? What you doin' here?"

"I'm here because of you, Pastor. Warden Cain thinks I was involved right there with you."

"What? Are you serious? I'm gonna write him a letter. Clear this whole thing up."

"Thank you. There's something else I need from you."

"What is it, Ronnie?"

"I need you to help me fight whatever it is that's going on in here. Will you pray with me?"

The prayers helped and the worst of the thoughts faded, but the next day I came face-to-face with the reality of life in Camp J. Nothing happened. For hours on end, I stood in my cell, watching, waiting. Still nothing happened.

I had no access to books and no hope of getting any. There was no TV, no yard time . . . Nothing but the walls of the six-by-nine cell, the thick bars across the front, and the dark, empty corridor beyond it.

The hours stretched and felt like days.

I talked to Pastor Norris when I could, but the gravity of despair was so strong it was hard to break free.

I mostly just lay on my bed and stared at the walls, trying to convince myself that they weren't really closing in on me.

———

I'd been in Camp J for almost a week when Pastor Norris shouted out to me. He told me he'd had a message back from Warden Cain about his letter and that the warden wasn't going to change his mind about me.

I wasn't surprised. When Warden Cain told me he was going to crush me if I failed the polygraph test, I had no doubt that he was completely serious. Now that I was in Camp J, he was going to hold me there.

I tried to get my head around how long I would be there. From what I could tell, Camp J still operated like it had when I worked there. Inmates were sent there for a period of six months. The rules and restrictions were hardest at the start, but after the first ninety days, things improved. Provided you behaved well for the first half, you would then be allowed to order food from the canteen. Ninety more days like that, and eventually you would be released back into General Population.

Six months. I might as well have been sentenced to six years. It felt like forever—an endless daily torture of nothing but blank walls and my own thoughts. I was grateful that I was able to keep my thoughts away from suicide, but each day was still a battle as I tried to figure out why God had let me end up there.

God knew I was telling the truth. He knew Warden Cain wasn't seeing things clearly. So why allow all this to continue? Why was God letting me rot in there? Why wasn't he putting things right?

I asked those questions a thousand times a day.

I never got any answers.

37 | FROM BAD DAYS TO LOW MOMENTS

Weeks passed. Nothing changed. Minutes felt like hours. Hours felt like days. From time to time one of the guards passing my cell would stop and do a double take, but eventually even that got predictable.

"Olivier? What you doin' in here?"

I'd explain things as simply as I could, and most of them would give the same response.

"That ain't right. Let me see what I can do to help you."

I'd smile and thank them, but I knew what would happen next. A few hours or days would pass, and they'd return, looking kind of down.

"Nothing I can do," they'd say. "Your file says you are to stay here until Warden Cain grants your release. I'm sorry, man. I just can't help you."

Gradually, my need to question God became a little less urgent. I stopped waiting on him for an explanation and shifted to telling myself that while it didn't make sense now, one day I'd understand. As soon as I hit that six-month date, I'd be out of Camp J and have all the answers I was looking for.

When I hit the ninety-day mark, I was told I was moving from level two to three. It meant I could access the canteen, and I tried to see the positives in it. *Just hold on*, I'd tell myself. *Six months, that's all. You've just gotta get to the end of this process, then this will all be over.*

———

September 17, 2011, came and went. I was still locked up.

For a few days I wondered whether they were measuring the six months from a different start date, but I was kidding myself. I wasn't being treated like any other inmate who'd been sent to Camp J, so I wasn't getting out at the same time as any other inmate in Camp J.

I tried to take the hit, to absorb the impact, but it was so hard. The walls started closing in all over again, and I could feel myself slipping.

Dawn had been asking to visit ever since I was sent to Camp J. I'd resisted at first, knowing far more restrictions were placed on visits there and not wanting to put either of us through it all. But as September ended, I had a change of heart.

The way things used to be, back when I was a Trusty, and even when I was in the Main Prison, visits were wonderful things. I could spend hours sitting around a table with Dawn in the visiting shed, holding the girls on my lap, talking and laughing and eating whatever good food was available that day. In Camp J, everything was different.

As soon as I walked into the Camp J visitor room and saw Dawn, I could feel myself starting to unravel. She stared at me, eyes wide and full of tears. The handcuffs and shackles made me walk slowly, and it was awkward to sit down at the booth I was shown to.

Dawn and I looked at each other, separated by a wire mesh screen.

It was hard to know what to say. After a long silence, I said the only words I could think of.

"I'm glad you didn't bring the girls."

Soon, Dawn's tears turned to sobs. We talked a little, but there was no escaping the fact that it was a horrible experience for her. For us both.

When it was over and I was back in my cell, I felt crushed all over again. Defeated. Abandoned. Forgotten.

———

Way back at the start of my time in Angola, when I was sent to the dungeon for having the handcuff shim, I tried to distract myself by replaying my favorite memories. I'd turn them over slowly, recalling all the senses possible, sucking every element that I could from them. I tried doing the same thing when I was in Camp J, and it would work from time to time. But it was hard to keep going like that, hour after hour, day after day, as the weeks edged by. Some of the memories that had helped me through my initial ten-day isolation were decades old and starting to fade. I was thirty-seven years old and had spent more than half my life in jail—twenty summers. Memories of my days of freedom felt like they belonged to somebody else.

I found myself drawn to more recent memories. Good times in Simmesport with Dr. Draper and his church, and happy memories from the visiting shed and church banquets in Angola. But what I settled on wasn't plates piled high with gumbo, empty fields flying by as we drove along the freeway, or even the feeling of holding Dawn's two girls. It was the wisdom I'd heard along the way.

"I don't have bad days, just bad moments," as one of my favorite pastors—Pastor Hicks—used to say. "I don't let those moments control my day or determine the way I'm going to feel for the next twenty-four hours."

Another time, Joyce Meyer had come to Angola to preach on the rodeo grounds. She was talking about Paul being in prison when he wrote to the church in Philippi. The conditions were terrible, with human waste flowing everywhere, but Paul was writing about joy. "You gotta think about what you're thinking about," Joyce said. "You don't have to be in prison *and* be depressed." Hearing that message had been such a turning point for me, inspiring me to look for the things I *could* enjoy while in prison.

There was another memory I turned to, from when I was working as an inmate minister in Camp J the first time. It was 2007, and Katrina had struck. Evacuees spread out across the state, and Angola was no different. We took in a number of prisoners from Orleans Parish, and I met a bunch of them at our church services. They were shocked by what they'd been through, and I remember telling one of them something that just came out of me: "There are always treasures and tragedies. When life gets hard, you've just got to search until you find the gold."

Years had passed since those times, but even in the darkness of Camp J, I was able to remember what it felt like to be inspired to grow closer to God. I was determined to go on a treasure hunt, to find the gold amid all the dungeon.

It was difficult at first, but I tried to focus on my thoughts. I tried to stop dwelling on the negative—stop feeding on the fear that I would spend years in Camp J. Those thoughts still came to me, but I didn't want to let them drag me down into a pit of depression and despair. One bad moment didn't need to turn into a whole bad day. Instead, I tried to take control, to think about things I knew would be good for me. I thought about Scripture, remembered worship songs that I liked. I thanked God for the good things and stopped trying to remind him about the bad.

Progress was slow. But on the plus side, I had a lot of time to practice.

———

Months passed, and still there was no sign of any change in Warden Cain's mind. The longer it went on, the more clearly I could see my position. I was locked away with no power to change the warden's thinking, and no real hope of ever getting out.

Every time I thought about this, I had to get to work. I'd remind myself that I wasn't powerless and that I wasn't at a loss for hope.

Right there in my cell, I could change things. And just like Paul in his cell, I had to leave everything else up to God.

Thinking about Paul was always good. He became my go-to mental distraction. I'd picture him in prison, filth flowing all around him, a great big smile on his face as he praised God. I'd remind myself that if he could do that, then I could find some joy myself.

One day it hit me: Paul wasn't just sitting in chains, praising. He was preaching. If Paul was preaching, why wasn't I?

So, I did.

From that moment on, I viewed Camp J not as my punishment but as my mission field. I made up my mind that anyone who came onto my tier was going to hear the gospel. I would tell them all about Jesus, no matter what.

This decision changed everything. I felt closer to God than I had at any point in my life. I was at peace, but I was also on fire. Though I still had low moments to battle through, I saw each day as an opportunity to say yes to God.

It wasn't just my perspective that changed. So many other guys were encouraged. And three became born-again.

38 | MY LIFE IS NOT IN WARDEN CAIN'S HANDS

Eyes closed. Breathing slow. I was sitting on my bed, somewhere between praying and sleeping. I'd been in Camp J for fifteen months, and I could soak up a good number of hours each day like this. Just resting. Keeping my mind clear. But this day was different. Instead of my mind being blank, I was somehow catching a prophetic sense of something that might one day happen to me. I was in New York, and the thought of it was enough to overwhelm me with joy.

I heard footsteps in the corridor outside my cell, and a familiar voice saying, "Which cell is he in?" There was an edge to the voice, a harshness it didn't usually have.

I opened my eyes and saw him stop in front of my bars.

"Ronald Olivier? Is that you?"

I smiled. "Pastor Cymbala." I hadn't seen Pastor Jim Cymbala from Brooklyn Tabernacle for months, not since before I left the Main Prison. He would come by the prison often and have all the guys featured in the *Miracle of Hope* video join him for a meal that Warden Cain had arranged for us. We would get full on food and fellowship and even be allowed to take some of the leftovers back to our dorms. It was good to see Pastor Cymbala again. I liked him being there. His presence reminded me of how things used to be.

"What are you doing here, Ronnie? You don't belong here."

I told him everything, just like I had a handful of times—the same story I'd told those security officers who were shocked to find

170

me in Camp J. He looked stunned as I talked, and more than a little upset.

"I'm going to talk to Warden Cain," he said when I was done with the backstory. I thought about telling him his idea wouldn't work, but it didn't seem right.

Not long after he left, I could hear footsteps in the corridor and the sound of Pastor Cymbala returning. I was sure I knew what he was going to say—that Warden Cain wasn't going to let me out anytime soon—and I was ready. I wasn't even feeling disappointed.

But that wasn't the message Pastor Cymbala had for me that day. What he said to me was enough to jolt me up out of my bed like I'd been hit with a thousand volts.

"Warden Cain's going to let you go, Ronnie."

———

Four months later I was lying down on my bed—the same bed in the same cell in the same camp I'd been in when Pastor Cymbala visited me before.

"Ronnie?"

"Pastor Cymbala!"

This time there was no long conversation between us. I was still stuck in the same cell, still waiting on Warden Cain to do what he'd said he'd do and let me go.

The one difference was Pastor Cymbala. The first time he was confused. Now he was furious.

"I'm gonna help you," he said. "I'm gonna get you out."

Later that day I was cuffed, shackled, and taken out of the cell and driven to Warden Cain's office. It was my first time in there, and my first time leaving Camp J in eighteen months. I was a little awed by all the people there—guys from Investigative Services, Warden Cain, and some chaplains I knew. I smiled at the one I knew best,

Chaplain Jim Rentz. He was an old guy in his eighties who'd been working at Angola for about three years. He was well respected in Christian circles inside and outside the prison. He'd often come to Camp J to encourage me, and I'd always known he was on my side.

But even the presence and smiles of Chaplain Rentz couldn't counterbalance the stares and tension the others were giving off. They were intimidating, and I could feel my head starting to spin.

Warden Cain took charge, asking me again to tell him what I knew about Pastor Norris and the cell phones. I knew what he wanted me to say. I could have easily lied and told him that I had known all along about the phones but that I hadn't said anything because I was trying to keep Pastor Norris from getting into further trouble. Pastor Norris had already completed his six months at Camp J and was back in General Population. But I wasn't going to lie. So I told him the exact same story I'd told him a year and a half earlier. I told him the truth.

Warden Cain sat back, and the room fell silent. I looked around and recognized one of the guys from Investigative Services as the same guy who had conducted the polygraph test. Beside him was a large case. I didn't need too many guesses to figure out what was in it.

The next person to speak wasn't Warden Cain but one of the chaplains. He took a step toward me. He looked angry. "Olivier, come on. Why are you lying? Why don't you just come clean?"

I stared back at him, not wanting to break eye contact. It was like being back in Camp D, being back on the street. He was trying to figure out if he could break me, and I was determined to prove that he couldn't.

Someone from Investigative Services spoke next, again accusing me of lying. As soon as he'd finished, another guy attacked. Each time the voices grew louder and the tension thicker. My heart was racing. I felt like the attack wasn't just on my truth or my character. It was an attack on my spirit. Sitting there, cuffed and shackled while all these guys were shouting at me, I wanted nothing more than to run.

"That's enough!"

The voice was loud. Loud enough to shut everyone up in an instant. But it wasn't Warden Cain who was yelling. It was Chaplain Rentz. He stared at every man in the room, especially Warden Cain.

"We're not here for this! We're here to clear his name. That's what we're here for. I believe he's telling the truth, and I ain't gonna let y'all attack him like this."

Warden Cain shrugged and nodded toward the guy with the briefcase. "Well, seems like we're gonna be doing another polygraph test."

I was feeling better this time than I had before. I kept my breathing calm and my head clear as the wires were attached and the first questions were put to me. I answered everything with nothing but total honesty.

When it was over, the officer conducting the test looked over at Warden Cain and shook his head.

Later that day I was back in Camp J. Same cell, same bed, same walls, same ceiling. But this time, I knew it was only temporary.

When I failed the polygraph test in Warden Cain's office, I thought the room might explode. But Chaplain Rentz took charge. He persuaded Warden Cain to give up on the test altogether and let me go. The warden didn't say much at first, but after a while it was clear that he couldn't think of a good enough reason to keep me. He even agreed to let me go to the Main Prison, back to a dorm and to the same job I'd been doing before, working as a clerk in the chapel. Not to mention, I was given my Trusty status back. I was fully restored.

It would take a couple of days to get everything in place, and I was okay with that. I needed time to think.

I was angry at first.

Angry that Warden Cain had been so wrong, so stubborn, and so uncaring. I believed he was born-again, that he and I were brothers in Christ, but I just couldn't figure out why he'd wanted to crush me in the first place. What was it about me that made him treat me so wrong?

Part of me could respect the way he had stuck to his convictions and held out for so long. But a bigger part of me couldn't understand why he was so convinced that his machine was more trustworthy than me. What had been going on during those eighteen months? Had he just forgotten about me, or was he really trying to crush me? And if Pastor Cymbala and Chaplain Rentz hadn't fought for me, how many more years would he have left me locked up down there, twenty-three hours a day?

All these questions were pointless, and the anger and bitterness felt toxic within me. I needed to forgive him, which I did, there on my bed in those final two days in Camp J. I also decided that when the two of us got to heaven, I'd be looking for him. When I found him, I'd get the answers I wanted.

As I let go of the anger and bitterness, I realized something else. Something that changed everything.

My life is not in Warden Cain's hands.

It never had been, and it never would be. Even if I got locked up in Camp J for the rest of my days, my life would still not be in Warden Cain's hands. It would only ever be in God's hands.

Warden Cain could never do anything to me that God hadn't allowed. God alone was the one I could trust. God alone was the one I needed to keep my eyes on.

PART 6

THE ROAD TO FREEDOM

39 | MY LIFE IS NOT IN CHICKEN GEORGE'S HANDS

Somewhere back around the time when I was running the streets, scientists were studying the brains and behavior of kids like me and reaching some dramatic conclusions. They found that the frontal lobe—the part responsible for appreciating risk and consequences—does not fully develop until a person is in their midtwenties. As juveniles we make rash decisions and take unnecessary actions we would steer clear of as adults. By age sixteen, we are not the men and women we will eventually become. This means that those of us who do commit crimes as juveniles stand a good chance of being rehabilitated as adults. It also means that imposing a lifetime of punishment for a crime committed when we are least able to appreciate risk and consequences is the very definition of cruel and unusual.

Even before I was locked up in Camp J, this new understanding of brain development was making an impact on the legal landscape. It had all started way back in 2005 with *Roper v. Simmons* and the Supreme Court's landmark decision that it is a violation of the Eighth Amendment to impose capital punishment for crimes committed while under the age of eighteen. Then it was *Graham v. Florida* in 2010, which led to a decision by the Supreme Court that juvenile offenders cannot be sentenced to life imprisonment without parole for non-homicide offenses. After that came the big one, *Miller v. Alabama*, in 2012. The Supreme Court ruled that it is unconstitutional to give a juvenile under the age of eighteen a mandatory life sentence without the possibility of parole, even when the offender had committed murder as a juvenile. It was a colossal ruling—one that instantly rendered sentences like mine unconstitutional and therefore illegal. More than three hundred juveniles had been sentenced to life without probation or parole in Angola, and we followed all these cases closely. We knew a change was coming. We just didn't know how long it would take to reach us.

It fell to each state to decide how to apply the Supreme Court's ruling. Louisiana chose what none of us juvenile lifers in Angola wanted: they decided not to apply it retroactively. While no other kid would be sentenced to life from 2012 onward, those of us who were already serving our now-unconstitutional life sentences were condemned to serve them until we died. Many people were discouraged by that, especially when we heard that it would likely be another ten or fifteen years before the United States Supreme Court would hear a case that dealt with the issue of retroactivity.

Those of us who were incarcerated weren't the only ones affected by the state's ruling. Our families suffered with us, just like always. When I phoned Dawn to tell her about it, she broke down completely. I stood holding the phone, listening to the sound of her screaming and howling. I'd never heard anyone in so much emotional pain.

When she calmed enough to breathe and come back to the phone, I tried to explain that this was just a setback. "Hold on," I said. "Something's gonna change one day. I believe it." Eventually someone would figure out a way to force a change in the law.

My optimism didn't work. Dawn had spent two decades of her life committed to a man behind bars. *Miller v. Alabama* released in her a hope that one day I might be free. To have that hope snatched away was just too much for her.

Our marriage didn't last much longer. Dawn got involved with another guy, and it was over. I knew how hard it had been for her to stay with me throughout my incarceration, and I told her that I really did appreciate all she had done for me. I told her I would continue to pray for her and be a dad to the girls if that's what they still wanted. All I needed from her was to make the divorce happen. She agreed, and by March 2015, the papers were signed and our divorce was complete.

My marriage was over, and the prospect of my release was fading to black. Hope was in short supply. But then Chicken George happened.

His real name was George Toca, but we all called him Chicken George on account of him being one of the scrawniest human beings we'd ever seen. He had been accused of murdering his best friend when he was just a kid, and he had always professed his innocence. Even the victim's family had testified that George and his friend were so inseparable that there was no way he could have done it. But the jury ruled against him, and the judge sent him away for life.

George had spent thirty years in Angola, fighting his case all along. Somehow, his case made it all the way to the Supreme Court, and a date was scheduled for sometime in 2015. If the court ruled in his favor concerning retroactivity, we'd all be going home. Of course, there were a lot of eager observers in Angola, and for a while Chicken George was the most popular man in the prison. But then the Louisiana DA played his cards. He offered Chicken George a deal: drop the case, and in return they would take back the life sentence and downgrade his charge to manslaughter. Since manslaughter carried a maximum sentence of twenty-one years at the time, Chicken George would be home free since he had already served three decades. All he had to do was sign the papers, and he'd be out of Angola within hours.

Chicken George came to see me when the rumors about the DA's deal started circulating. He looked even skinnier and scrawnier than usual.

"Would you pray for me?" he asked. "I don't know what to do."

We prayed awhile. Then we talked.

"There's a lot of weight on you, Chicken. A lot of weight."

"I know. My mama's sick and she ain't got much time left. My family all want me to take the deal and get back home quick. If I stay and fight the case, she might not be alive when I get out. But I want to help people in here too. I don't want to leave y'all."

"Listen, man. I learned something back in Camp J. I learned that my life is not in Warden Cain's hands, and it ain't in Chicken George's hands either. You don't decide the facts of my life. Only God does. You need to make this decision according to what's best for you. Whatever you decide, I'll support you."

He took the deal. The case disappeared from the Supreme Court's diary, and we all had to adjust to the reality that our one shot of forcing Louisiana to make *Miller v. Alabama* retroactive was over. Maybe, just maybe, we might get another case before the Supreme Court one day, but it wouldn't be anytime soon.

For a while, a lot of people were real mad with Chicken George. Thankfully the authorities got him out of Angola as quick as they'd promised to. If he'd been in there for any longer, there's a good chance someone would have killed him.

———

Aside from his skinny frame and the fact that he, too, had been sentenced to life without parole for a crime he had committed as a juvenile, Henry Montgomery was nothing like Chicken George. Everybody seemed to know George in Angola, and he was one of those guys who was impossible not to like. But Henry Montgomery was different. He was quiet and reserved, walking around like he thought nobody would notice him if he didn't make a sound or disturb anyone. He didn't have many friends, or any at all as far as I could tell. He'd been there for decades when I'd first arrived, and I don't think I'd said two words to him the whole time I'd been in Angola. But Henry

Montgomery was the one who changed my life and the lives of all those others like me.

Three months after the DA persuaded Chicken George to withdraw his case from the Supreme Court, a new rumor went around Angola. Henry Montgomery's case was going to be heard in the Supreme Court. It was shocking news, and a bunch of people didn't believe it at first. But on January 25, 2016, it happened. The Supreme Court ruled in Henry Montgomery's favor. Finally, the *Miller v. Alabama* ruling was to be applied retroactively in Louisiana and all other states.

40 | THE RODEO

If there's one thing Angola is known for, apart from its being a former slave plantation that was once regarded as the most brutal prison in the country, it's the rodeo. Every Sunday in October and over the third weekend in April, Louisiana State Penitentiary becomes home to one of the wildest things you've ever seen as thousands of visitors flock to witness the inmate-run rodeo.

All the usual rodeo events happen, from Buddy Pickup to Cowboy Poker—where four inmates sit around a table while a bull charges toward them, and the last one to leave his chair collects the money. In Guts and Glory, the ring is full of inmates all trying to get close enough to a raging bull to pull off the pendant that's tied between his horns. The winner gets $500, and if nobody wins that day, then the prize money rolls over to the next day. For a bunch of inmates earning between four and twenty cents an hour working for the prison, the idea of walking away with a few hundred dollars is tantalizing. The guys will take a lot of risks to win.

Like any rodeo, it isn't just about what goes on in the ring at Angola. As many as seventy booths sell everything from food to hobby crafts—Asian food, Southern food, fried Snickers, and anything else a person could want, all run by different prison clubs. And the crafts the inmates sell—which have all been made by them too—are impressive. People drive for hours to buy leather belts and purses, gun cabinets, and rocking chairs with different football team designs cut into the back.

You have to be a Trusty to have any contact with the public, and every person selling their items on a concession needs a staff member to be their sponsor. The sponsor alone handles the money, making sure it goes directly to the relevant club account.

For the most talented craftsmen, the rodeo represents a significant opportunity to raise some money. One guy I knew bought his kid a car with the money he'd earned there. But for most guys, the real appeal of the rodeo isn't the money or the adrenaline surge of being in the ring. It's the chance to meet women.

———

I was working on the alligator sausage concession one October weekend. My divorce from Dawn had been finalized several months before, but I was one of the few guys who wasn't looking for romance that day. The State of Louisiana had been dragging its heels on how to deal with *Miller v. Alabama*, and I had more than enough going on with my own case. The last thing I wanted was to drag someone else into it with me.

So I was keeping myself to myself that day. My friend Bossier, on the other hand, was in full-on hunter mode. And when he told me he'd met someone called Special-K and that she was as fine as any woman he'd ever seen in his entire life.

"I'm telling you, man, you gotta meet her. She's gonna visit next month."

I was skeptical, but Bossier was happy, so I just smiled and told him I was pleased for him.

Next month, it happened just as he said it would. This girl Kristen showed up, and Bossier had me come to the visiting shed to say hi. We talked for five or ten minutes, prayed a little, and then I stood up to leave.

"Are you involved with anyone?" Kristen asked.

"No, ma'am. And I'm not trying to be. I'm fresh out of a divorce, and I'm not ready for a relationship."

She nodded and smiled. I left and didn't think any more about it.

Next month, Bossier was even more excited. It was December, and he'd arranged for Kristen to come for a "Christmas special"—a double-length visit lasting eight hours. Again, I told him I was pleased for him.

"That's just it," he said. "Kristen's not coming alone. She's bringing her cousin to meet you too. You get to spend the whole day in the visiting shed with us."

I was less than happy. I'd meant what I said to Kristen before: I really was not looking for anyone. The thought of spending a whole day making polite conversation with a stranger was not my idea of fun.

Then something unexpected happened.

In Angola, instead of inmates receiving physical mail, a basic computer terminal called KIOSK was set up in each dorm that allowed us to send and receive emails. When someone from the outside created an account, their name would pop up on the inmate's mailing list. Well, a week before my daylong blind date, I saw a new name appear on my list: *Teirsen*. I'd never met anyone called Teirsen before, and I was pretty sure I'd never even heard the name. But I figured it must be the person Special-K was bringing along, so I sent her a message.

Hey. I'm Ronnie Olivier and I'm an inmate here in Angola.
I enjoyed meeting Special-K last month, and I'm looking
forward to meeting you on Saturday. Bye, Ronnie.

Next day, when I was checking my email, a reply came in. She told me a little about herself—including the fact that she was divorced and had two children. I thought it was interesting that she'd write that straight off, so I was quick with my reply. I asked her for a photo so I would recognize her when she arrived.

By this time, I was checking my emails every half hour. When she replied, I couldn't stop looking at the screen.

Leekie was also doing a stretch in Angola back then, and the next time I saw him, I made sure we were near a computer so I could get his opinion.

"What do you think?" I asked. "I'm confused. From what she's written so far, she's articulate and smart, and her face is beautiful too. But why did she send me a shot that's just from the neck up? You think she's like three hundred pounds or something?"

Leekie studied the image like a detective at a crime scene. "Nah, no way is she fat," he announced when he was finished, tapping the screen with his finger. "Look at her neck."

I stared. It all felt too good to be true.

———

By the time visiting day came around, Teirsen and I had exchanged a few more emails and I'd practically memorized every word of them. I spotted her the moment she walked into the visiting shed and was ready for a hug as she approached the table where Bossier and I were standing. She diverted away from me at the last minute. Not a good start.

Bossier and Kristen were locked in conversation right from the beginning, laughing and getting close to each other, looking like they'd been dating for a year. Teirsen looked nervous.

"Don't worry," I said. "This is the safest place in the prison. Nothin' is going to happen to you in here."

She relaxed a little, and we started talking. We talked a lot, but because the shed was full and loud, I had to move my seat forward to get close enough to hear her. Every time I moved closer, she moved back. I felt like I was chasing her around the table. Not a good sign at all.

There was a moment's silence after we'd been talking an hour or so. For once I didn't fill it. I could tell Teirsen had something to say, so I waited for her to speak.

"I'm interested, Ronnie. Why are you in prison?"

I took a breath and told her the truth. I didn't try to downplay any part of it or make excuses. I wanted her to know everything up front. If what I'd done was going to be a problem for her, I wanted to find that out as soon as possible.

When I'd finished, she stared at me. "You were how old?"

"I was sixteen when I killed him."

"What? They put kids in prison?"

There was a lot I could have said right then, especially about my early days in Angola, but it didn't feel right. The moment passed, and the subject changed. Teirsen started telling me about her own life— about her two kids, her job, and her tight-knit family.

I was mesmerized. For the first time in my life, I wanted to hold on to every word I was hearing. I felt like I could trust her, like I could listen to her speak all day and never get tired. I felt like . . . like I was talking to my future wife.

I checked myself. This all scared me.

I've been divorced for only a few months. I'm vulnerable. Am I just reaching out because I'm hurt?

We kept talking all day. When it was time for her to go, I played what I was sure was going to be a pretty good card.

"I got you a gift. It's not much, but you know . . . Here it is."

I handed over a bag with two wrapped packages.

She smiled as she opened the first one. "Hey, a Bible."

"It's a study Bible," I added. "It's great for—"

"Study?"

"Yeah."

She turned to the second gift. "And what's this?" She pulled the paper off and stared at the cute little stuffed bear.

"A guy in here makes them from pillowcases," I said. I'd just rushed to buy it that morning, and I hadn't had time to have a good look at it myself.

"Do you like it?"

"I do," she said, turning it around so I could see. "It's just . . ."

The bear was holding a sign. It said, "I Miss You."

All the air went out of the room.

"Oh, Teirsen, I'm sorry. I didn't know it said that."

"Nope, it's fine. Really."

———

A week later, three days before Christmas, I was downloading some music on the KIOSK when my inbox lit up.

It was Teirsen. She was wishing me a merry Christmas and telling me that she enjoyed our day together. But she was also telling me she wasn't going to be able to visit anymore or send more emails.

I'd taken a lot of punches and kicks in my younger years, but this blow hurt more than any of them. I'd told her all about how Christmas was especially difficult for me, how I went back and replayed the events every year. She knew I was dealing with that, yet she sent me this. It didn't make sense.

I found Leekie and told him everything.

"My heart is broken, man."

Leekie wasn't listening. "Slim, she'll be back. She never experienced nobody like you before. I'm telling you, man, she gotta come back."

"I don't know, Leekie. I'm thinking it's over. This was the one shot I had at the perfect woman. Now she's gone."

I didn't know if I could survive Christmas that year. I didn't care about the food or the gifts or anything else. All I wanted was to get through to the other side. I was done with 2015. The year couldn't end soon enough.

But the year had one more surprise.

An email, early on Christmas Day.

From Teirsen.

41 | THE SPIRITUAL GYM

Teirsen and I reached a mutual agreement. We decided to be friends, to stay connected and be sources of spiritual encouragement to each other. Nothing more, nothing less.

It was just what I needed. The court had ruled that *Miller v. Alabama* was retroactive, and the state decided the best way forward was to create a new law. Now inmates with life sentences for crimes committed as juveniles were eligible for parole after twenty-five years. With my quarter-century milestone approaching, I was preparing to engage in the long process of applying for parole. None of it would be simple, and none of it would be quick. It was going to be a long, hard battle, and the last thing I wanted was to force someone else to suffer through it with me.

I also needed to learn how to receive. I'd been working in ministry for so many summers, so many years. I'd been constantly giving out, serving others. Having come from a family of generous people, I wasn't much good at receiving, and prison had only made it worse. One of the keys to surviving those earliest years had been caution. It had been vital that I always remain on my guard, responding carefully whenever anyone showed generosity or kindness. I constantly asked myself what they wanted from me in return, to determine whether saying yes to what appeared to be a simple act of friendship was something I would end up regretting later.

That way of thinking had eased over time, but two decades into my sentence, a part of me still held on to a mindset that took pride in not depending on anyone. Resilience and independence had helped me through eighteen months of isolation in Camp J, but they were not going to be much help if I wanted to have a true friendship with Teirsen.

Learning to receive was one of the hardest lessons, but I'd made plenty of other progress in my life already. The more I looked back on my spiritual journey in prison, the more I noticed the distance traveled. At the start I was a true infant: messy, weak, and unable to really do anything for myself. I was a cussing Christian in those early days, and I needed a lot of help, guidance, feeding, and cleaning up. But in time—thanks to Bishop Tannehill, Tony, and Pastor Joe—that all changed. I came to see that prison was teaching me some powerful lessons. It was like a gym, but instead of weights, bars, and other machines that offer resistance and help build muscle, the spiritual gym of prison was full of difficult people and frustrating circumstances that challenged me to grow in my spiritual gifts.

Patience, for example. After Camp J, with all the potential fallout of *Miller v. Alabama* still in the air, I was tempted to get frustrated when change wasn't coming quick enough. I prayed for more patience and found myself presented with lots of opportunities to practice it. I noticed that I had to spend a lot of time waiting at gates while security officers slowly got around to letting me through. Previously I would have let myself get riled up by whoever was holding me up, but having asked for more patience, my perspective changed. I saw those few minutes standing in a corridor as an opportunity, not a barrier. I'd make the choice to wait well and happily, telling myself that this was all part of my spiritual workout—that I was building muscle, minute by minute.

There's a lot of waiting in prison and a lot of unhappy, awkward men, so in addition to patience, I also got to practice being more loving to people. One time I asked God to teach me how to love, and within days, someone moved into the dorm with me. He was rude, selfish, aggressive, and easily offended. Altogether, he was just about the hardest person to love that I'd ever met, and I was in the bed next to him.

Great! This is my gym. What does it say in the Bible about it being easy to love someone who loves you—that even the sinners do that? It's time to love my enemy.

Meekness was another lesson. Where I grew up, meekness was seen as weakness, and weakness could get you in serious trouble. I saw that played out in Angola so often, and for the longest time I saw no need for meekness at all. But as the years passed and I studied the Bible more, I concluded that meekness is not weakness. It's strength under control. It's about transferring your rights, taking authority over anger or pain, and choosing to respond in a better way. Inmates get offended regularly and feel as though they have a right to respond in a certain manner, nearly always with violence. Meekness means putting that right down and choosing a better option, like a soft word or walking away. Proverbs 15:1 lays it all out for us: "A soft answer turneth away wrath: but grievous words stir up anger."

When Mama got banned from the visiting shed and stopped depositing so much money in my account, I found myself in the spiritual gym. No more buying the things I wanted from the canteen, no more going to the store and coming back with items I liked the look of but didn't need—items like soups, chips, tuna fish, and cookies. I had to learn to be content with the little I had.

Training is painful. When you first start to work a muscle you've hardly ever used before, the pain is even worse. But whether you're in the physical gym or the spiritual gym, if there's no pain or discomfort, you're probably not making any real progress. And just as you can tell when someone's been working out physically, so, too, can you see the benefits when someone's been working out spiritually. It just shows.

Reflecting on my spiritual journey was helpful as Teirsen and I kept in contact with each other and offered encouragement and support. But I had another reason for wanting to be as spiritually fit as possible: finally, I was heading back to court.

42 | FALLING

For months, Teirsen and I had been committed to staying on that simple path we had set for ourselves early on. We were going to encourage each other spiritually, to be nothing but positive forces in each other's lives. We were taking it easy, whatever *it* was.

Then the rodeo happened.

Teirsen came and brought her sister, Tyra. She'd told me a little about Tyra before, but it was only when I met her in person that I realized why Teirsen wanted us to meet.

Tyra is like Teirsen on steroids. She's whip-smart, talks in complete paragraphs, and has a level of insight and understanding that I've not seen in many others. She's also warm and can talk to anyone. I could tell within minutes of meeting her that she was neither intimidated by me nor judgmental of what I'd done. She was just being herself, curious and excited to meet this guy her sister was friends with.

We talked for hours, and when it was time for them to go, I asked Tyra whether she would mind if I prayed for her. She said it would be fine, and I thanked God for the chance to meet his daughter. Then I asked that he bless her and her family and keep them safe.

When we'd all said amen, Tyra looked at me. "Ronnie, do you mind if I pray with you?"

"Of course not."

She prayed out loud, her voice quickly starting to crack. When she was done and I opened my eyes, she had tears on her cheeks.

Teirsen, meanwhile, was staring at her sister. I'd never seen anyone look quite so shocked.

We said goodbye and I didn't think a whole lot of it, but a few days later, Teirsen emailed.

She told me Tyra had never prayed out loud for anyone before. Ever.

She told me there was only one person's approval she ever really sought in this world: Tyra's.

And she told me about a dream she'd had. A dream in which I came home.

What she didn't say was what this all added up to. But she didn't need to. I was falling in love, and I was sure she was too.

43 | MY LIFE IS NOT IN HER HANDS

I had hurdles to clear—like finding a lawyer, raising the $5,000 to pay the lawyer, filing a motion to correct my sentence, then waiting for the State of Louisiana to agree to my case—but eventually, one by one, I cleared them all. Thanks to the generosity and commitment of my family and the hard work of my lawyer, I was finally going to get my day in court. I even had a date: November 2016.

Only it wasn't quite that simple. My case wouldn't be decided with just one day in court. Even though it had taken a single day for me to be tried and found guilty, the process to correct my sentence—which was now illegal—would take a lot more time and a lot more work on my part. My lawyer would need to convince the judge of the merits of my case, and if we were successful, then I would have to apply for—and be granted—parole. There would be months between each stage in the process, and no clear timeline to follow. It would fall on me to provide evidence that I was reformed and ready to be released. There were no guarantees that I would be successful. Several inmates in Angola had been sentenced as juveniles like I had, but they hadn't been released. With all these hurdles still ahead of me, I could only hope for things to move smoothly without any unforeseen delays or problems.

———

For more than a year my lawyer had been working on my case. He'd been talking with the DA and judges, and I had been to court several times. But I had never gotten a full hearing. At one point the DA had even considered reducing my sentence to manslaughter, which carried a twenty-one-year maximum. Given that I'd exceeded that, I could have been sent straight home. But when the Louisiana Supreme Court ruled *Miller* wasn't retroactive, that deal disappeared like the morning mist. I went back to Angola, back to waiting.

It felt like the state was running a filibuster play. My lawyer was not happy, so he took my case first to the state's high court and eventually to federal court. It worked, and the state was given ninety days to give me a hearing. The writ handed down by the federal court stipulated that if the state failed to rule on my case within the ninety days, I would be released.

As I walked into Orleans Parish Section F courtroom in New Orleans on October 7, 2016, I felt different from the way I'd felt on all the other court dates. One way or the other, I could see the end in sight.

My sister was in court that day. So was Teirsen, Chaplain Rentz, and a whole lot of other family members. But I wasn't focusing on any of them. Or on my lawyer, the judge, or the DA. My attention was locked on the woman sitting across the aisle from me on the front row. She was staring at me.

I didn't want to give the wrong impression or appear intimidating in any way, so I was careful not to look directly at her. Instead, I stared at my cuffs and shackles—which I had never gotten used to—or at the files and folders my lawyer had lined up on the table in front of him. I let myself glance over in the direction of the woman from time to time, only for the briefest possible moment. She was always staring back at me. Eyes locked like they were made of steel.

"This is all messed up," said my lawyer when the start time came and went. He looked and sounded stressed, not at all like a lawyer who thought he had a winning hand. "There's a new development. The victim's sister showed up. That's her there."

He gestured, and I looked over. She was still staring. "That's not his sister," I said. "That's his mother. I remember her face from my trial."

I thought back to the conversation I'd had with the pastor from New Orleans years earlier. This woman had taken his call but had not been willing to talk to me. Now I was in the same room as her, feeling her gaze, sensing my lawyer's fear that she could derail everything. In many ways, this looked bad. Hopeless, even.

And yet, I'd been in the gym. I had some faith muscles.

I leaned over to my lawyer. "Would you find out if she would be willing to talk to me?"

He looked at me, then back over at her. I couldn't tell whether he thought it was a crazy-bad idea or a crazy-good one. Not that I spent too much time worrying about it. I was praying hard.

My lawyer went to talk with the judge and the DA. I kept my eyes down, blocking out the blur of the courtroom. It was just me, praying.

Five minutes later my lawyer was back.

"DA says she doesn't want to talk," he said, his voice low. "Whatever she says here today she will say on the stand."

"Oh, Lord," I whispered. I felt like a hand was closed tight around my throat, choking all the air and all the hope and all the faith out of me. "Please . . . my life is not in her hands. Is it?"

44 | THE PLAN

A procedural issue meant the court hearing in November 2016 never even started. I was taken out the back door to wait for my ride back to Angola. It was a heavy blow, and I was wrestling against doubt and fear, trying to hold on to this sense I had that God was going to get me out somehow.

Meanwhile, out in the corridor in front of the courtroom, a crowd of people waited. My sister Penny was there, trying to make sense of everything just like everybody else was. She'd been at the original trial, and like me, she'd recognized the victim's mother instantly. So she approached her, introduced herself as my sister, and said the one thing she wanted to say more than anything else.

"As a family we never had a chance to express our condolences for your son. We want to apologize for what my brother did. Ronnie's changed so much in all these years, but that's neither here nor there. We just want you to know we're sorry."

The mother didn't say much, and they parted.

A few minutes later, while Penny was heading out toward the exit, a reporter from the *Times-Picayune* approached, asking if she wanted to do a story.

My lawyer was there, and he was quick to shut it down. The reporter wasn't surprised, but she said something that stunned Penny.

"The lady came here to forgive your brother."

I was back in Angola by the time I heard all this from Penny. She was feeling encouraged by the reporter's remark, but I didn't feel the same way. It confused me. The fierce stare the woman was giving me in the courtroom just didn't line up with what the reporter had said.

All I could do was pray. The more I prayed, the more I started to believe that maybe it wasn't so bad after all. Perhaps the reporter had been telling the truth. Perhaps there was room for a little hope.

The hearing was rescheduled for December 8, just within the ninety-day deadline the federal court had set. I was ready to try my best to convince the judge I was worthy of release, just like I had been before, but I was also ready to face the victim's mother. If she stared or not, I wouldn't mind. I sat on my bench on the front row, cuffed and shackled as always, and ran through what I wanted to do and say. I had a plan. I was ready to put it into action.

The court filled up, the start time approached, and I saw my plan go up in smoke. The lady wasn't there. My family was there, as were Teirsen and Chaplain Rentz. But the victim's mother was nowhere to be seen. I strained to see if she was sitting at the back or lurking in the doorway, but she wasn't. The one person my plan depended on had decided to stay home. I dropped my head and started praying, but it was hard to focus. This wasn't how I'd hoped it would go, and I was starting to fear this was yet another bad sign.

I tried to tell myself it was okay. I reminded myself of the mantra that had seen me through so many challenges. That my life was not in her hands. Only God had control, and he was someone I could always rely on.

"Sit up," my lawyer said quietly. I did what I was told and looked up to see the DA approaching.

"She's on her way," the DA said to my lawyer. "Just a little longer."

I went back to praying. In some ways I didn't mind whether she came. I wanted to be free, to get all of this over with, to move on to a parole hearing, and to eventually go home. But on a deeper level, I knew there was something more important than all that. Something I needed more than parole.

I looked up when I sensed a change in the courtroom's atmosphere. My sister was standing up, waving at the door. The victim's mother had arrived. She walked over to Penny, and after they'd talked awhile, the lady went directly to the DA and said a few words. He got up, walked over to the judge, then to my lawyer. Finally, the message was delivered to me:

"She wants to talk to you. You've only got a few minutes though."

The DA brought the lady over and sat beside her in the row behind me. It was a little awkward to turn around and face her, but I did my best.

Her arms were folded. The same steely look I'd noticed last time we were in court still filled her eyes.

I took a deep breath. The only time she'd heard me speak was at the trial, twenty-five years earlier. On that day I'd denied everything. I'd stood up and told the court I was not guilty of murdering her son. I'd told the court I was there that night, but I didn't have a weapon and didn't have anything to do with the murder. I was innocent, I'd said. His death had nothing to do with me.

"Ma'am . . ." I could feel my voice trembling inside me. I felt lightheaded, as if the air was thin. "Ma'am, I take full responsibility for the death of your son."

45 | "I'M PROUD OF YOU"

She unfolded her arms and leaned closer to me.

Everything else faded to the background. The noise of the courtroom, the bite of the metal in my wrists and ankles, even the DA sitting next to her. None of it held any interest to me. None of it mattered. The only thing I could focus on was her. The mother whose grief I caused. The mother whose son I killed.

I tried to carry on talking, but I started crying instead. I tried to stop, to let myself speak, but nothing would stop the tears. Through the blur, I could see her sobbing too.

"It was stupid," I said when I eventually caught my breath. "It was idiotic. I was very impulsive. I wasn't thinking. I just reacted. It shouldn't have happened. Ma'am, I just ask that you forgive me. I pray that somehow you could find somewhere in your heart to forgive me."

She looked at me. The same eyes that had stared at me from across the courtroom, but without the steel, without as much of the pain either. "I don't hate you. But what you did completely changed my life. You know, my son being killed? But I forgive you."

The planets shifted. My heart found a different rhythm. I wanted to stay in this moment, to not lose it, but there was something else I needed to say. I hadn't planned it, but the words were rushing up and tumbling out of me before I could even question them.

"Ma'am, I think it's only right that you know what really happened. There was talk throughout the trial that me and your son got into it because of a female. And I say, ma'am, none of that happened.

There was no female involved. I never knew your son, never spoke with him. The altercation was with the other guy I shot that night. Your son just happened to be with him."

I could have said more about Starter jackets and being spun around when I was getting on the bus, but I had said enough. I didn't want to give the impression that I was trying to shift any of the blame. Because it was all on me. Every bit of it.

"It should never have happened," I said again. "I shouldn't have had a gun, and I want to say again that it was the most stupid, idiotic decision I ever made in my life. I know that I not only took your son from you, but I took Christmas from you too. I'm sure Christmas ain't never been the same for you."

"Yeah, you're right. It never has been."

"Ma'am, I want you to know that I've been praying for y'all. And I pray that somehow God would restore Christmas to you."

"Thank you. I appreciate that."

The tears were still falling for both of us, but neither of us spoke. I'd said enough, but it seemed like she wanted to say something else.

"It's funny," she said, wiping her face. "What I didn't know until after my son died was that he had a baby son already. When my boy died, I raised his son. I wanted to bring him here to meet you today. I talked to my whole family about you, and they forgive you. I really want him to meet you."

"Thank you." The tears started getting heavier again, but I could see her smile. "I would like to meet him, if I get out."

She shook her head just a little. "Not *if* you get out. When."

The DA leaned in and said something about the judge being ready for the hearing to commence. I heard the words, but they didn't mean much to me. I was too busy staring at my hands. I could have sworn that someone had just taken my cuffs and shackles off. I felt free— freer than I'd ever felt at any point in my life. I was light, with not a single burden on me. Whether the judge set me free that day or sent me back to Camp J for the rest of my days, I really didn't mind. I'd been forgiven. That was all that mattered.

The court hearing started, but I was only ever vaguely aware of what was going on. At some point Chaplain Rentz took the stand and told the judge about some of the things I'd done while I was in Angola and at Avoyelles. Penny spoke, too, followed by the victim's mother. She told the court exactly what she'd told me in private. That the pain hurt so bad. That she forgave me. That she wished me well.

The DA even spoke up for me. He said that in all his career he'd never heard somebody take ownership for their actions like I had. He said people always had some excuse, always had someone else to blame. But he applauded me for saying what I had said, for owning what I had done.

During the hearing, the judge spent a long time reading through the portfolio I had prepared. It was almost as thick as a phone book—a complete record of everything I had done since I was incarcerated. It included my GED certificate, transcripts from Bible college, reports on groups I had led, letters from friends and family, and so much more besides.

"I took all these things into account," she said after calling me to stand before her. "I do believe, Mr. Olivier, you are a person who was capable of being rehabilitated, and I do believe you have been rehabilitated . . . I have decided to grant your motion."

I closed my eyes. I could hear the noise and the cheers and the tears. Inside me, all was still. I was breathing in a miracle.

When the courtroom was quiet again, the judge continued.

"I'm very, very proud of you. I am. I really am. I don't think I've ever seen a portfolio like this. I'm very proud of you."

"Thank you, Your Honor."

My hearing was the last of the day, so I knew almost everyone in the courtroom. When the judge declared the hearing over, I was ready to be taken out the back as usual and transferred to Angola, but she said I could take a few moments to talk with my family.

I turned to face them. They were all there, everyone I loved in the world. They moved toward me, a great ocean of love coming my way.

But among them, pushing forward to the head of the crowd, was someone not related to me. Someone I'd only just spoken to for the first time that day.

She reached me first. Put her hands on my shoulders. Stared me straight in the eyes.

"I think you're gonna do good," she said. "But just do me a favor."

"Yes, ma'am. Anything at all."

"Man, don't pick up no gun."

"No, ma'am. You never have to worry about that. I won't pick one up. Ever."

She smiled and nodded. Then she turned and left.

46 | GOD'S MOST PRECIOUS TREASURES

Even though the judge had told me she hoped I wouldn't have to wait too long for my parole board hearing, I assumed it would take time. With three hundred inmates affected by *Miller v. Alabama*, the parole board was busier than ever. Even though I'd been resentenced and was now officially eligible for parole, I would have to wait my turn.

Not everyone who was eligible was granted parole. Inmates had to meet certain requirements that were easy to identify, such as serving twenty-five years of a sentence or earning a GED. Other requirements—such as completing some programs and acquiring skills that would be relevant to life outside—were a little more complicated to discern. People who had spent years doing nothing in Angola were now desperately trying to create a portfolio to convince the board they were genuinely reformed and ready for release. The parole boards were getting wise to all this, though, and once again I was grateful to the old guy in Hunts who had told me to sign up for every program possible. My portfolio was good, and it showed that my change was authentic. But the line ahead of me was long. Someone told me it could take months for my hearing to be scheduled. I feared it might take years.

I settled down to life in Angola, spending my days working in the Chaplain's Department before returning to Dormitory Unit Ash 3, Bed #22 to sleep. I threw myself into church ministry, where a lot of people were feeling bitter about the number of inmates being released thanks to *Miller v. Alabama*, especially those who were waiting for their shot at parole like I was.

"We are a family," I told them, over and over. "We're the body of Christ. If a foot gets out, then it might be the hand's turn next. We should be celebrating when good things happen to each other."

Whenever someone was released, we'd have him run victory laps around the church. We would stand up and cheer him on, and some of us would run with him.

"Who's next?" I'd yell. "Who's next?"

But it was Bill Yount's prophecy that really helped. I'd read it out over and over, reminding people of the vision of an exodus of inmates going out from the prisons to do God's work in the communities where the church was struggling to make an impact.

"We're seeing it, ain't we?" I'd say whenever we talked about the prophecy. "This is Angola's exodus. Don't tell me what God can't do."

God's Most Precious Treasures

by Bill Yount

It was late and I was tired, wanting to go to sleep, but God wanted to talk; it was about midnight, but it dawned on me that God does not sleep. His question made me restless, "Bill, where on earth does man keep his most priceless treasures and valuables?" I said, "Lord, usually these treasures like gold, silver, diamonds, and precious jewels are kept locked up somewhere out of sight, usually with guards and security to keep them under lock and key." God spoke, "Like man, My most valuable treasures on earth are also locked up." I then saw Jesus standing in front of seemingly thousands of prisons and jails. The Lord said, "These have almost been destroyed by the enemy, but these ones have the greatest potential to be used and to bring forth glory to My name. Tell My people I am going this hour to the prisons to activate the gifts and callings that lie dormant in these lives that were given before the foundation of the earth. Out from these walls will come forth an Army of Spirituals, who will have power to literally kick down the gates of hell and overcome satanic powers that are holding many of My own people bound in My own house.

"Tell My people that great treasure is behind these walls, in these forgotten vessels. My people must come forth and touch these ones, for a mighty anointing will be unleashed upon these for future victory in My Kingdom. THEY MUST BE RESTORED!"

I then saw the Lord step up to the prison doors with a key. One key fit every lock and the gates began to open. I then heard and saw great explosions, which sounded like dynamite going off behind the walls. It sounded like all out spiritual warfare. Jesus turned and said, "Tell My people to go in now and pick up the spoil and rescue these." Jesus then began walking in and touching inmates who were thronging Him. Many being touched instantly began to have a golden glow come over them. God spoke to me, "THERE'S THE GOLD!" Others had a silver glow around them. God said, "THERE'S THE SILVER!"

Like slow motion, they began to grow into what appeared to be giant knights in armor-like warriors. They had on the entire armor of God and every piece was solid and pure gold! Even golden shields! When I saw the golden shields, I heard God say to these warriors: "Now go and take what satan has taught you and use it against him. Go and pull down the strongholds coming against MY church. The spiritual giants then started stepping over the prison walls with no one to resist them, and they went immediately to the very front line of the battle with the enemy. I saw them walk right past the church; and big-name ministers known for their power with God were surpassed by the giant warriors, like David going after Goliath! They crossed the enemy's line and started delivering many of God's people from the clutches of satan while demons trembled and fled out of their presence. No one, not even the church, seemed to know who these spiritual giants were or where they come from. All you could see was the armor, the golden armor of God, from head to foot, and the shields of gold were there. The shields were restored to God's House and there was great victory and rejoicing.

I also saw silver, precious treasures, and vessels being brought in. Beneath the gold and silver were the people that nobody knew: REJECTS OF SOCIETY, STREET PEOPLE, THE OUTCAST, THE POOR, and THE DESPISED. These were the treasures that were missing from His House.

In closing, the Lord said, "If My people want to know where they are needed, tell them they are needed in the STREETS, the HOSPITALS, the MISSIONS, and PRISONS. When they come there, they will find Me and the next move of My Spirit, and they will be judged by My Word in Matthew 25:42–43, "For I was hungry and you gave Me no meat; I was thirsty and you gave Me no drink: I was a stranger and you took Me not in: naked, and you clothed Me not: sick, and in prison, and you visited Me not."

The penal system in the United States is not broken. It's working exactly the way it was designed to work. It is designed for failure. It is designed to target mostly Black and Brown people and treat them worse than whites. It is designed to lock people away for decade after decade, to suffocate life rather than rehabilitate it. It is designed to treat people as animals.

But I am not an animal.

I was never an animal.

I was a foolish kid who made terrible choices, and I deserved to be punished for them.But even though the penal system would have happily left me locked away until I died and called it justice, God never gave up on me. He had other plans for me, his most precious treasure. Just like he does for every single one of us.

There's so much injustice woven into our justice system, but it can change. It'll take a lot of work, and a lot of good people will need to say yes to what God invites them into. But it can happen. It will happen. It's happening already.

47 | "ONE GUY I WOULD DIE FOR"

It took almost two years before I finally got a date to appear before the parole board. Part of the delay was down to the volume of cases ahead of me, but despite all the time I had to think it over, trying to figure out what my life would look like if I was granted parole wasn't as easy as one might expect.

My initial plan was to move to Brooklyn and take up the offer of a job at Brooklyn Tabernacle Church. Pastor Jim Cymbala had been looking out for me for years, and I loved the idea of working within his church and learning from him as I'd learned from Dr. Draper. But Louisiana law wouldn't let me move out of state as a new parolee, so I had to find an alternative plan. Enter Chaplain Rentz. He had been as influential in my life as Pastor Cymbala and Dr. Draper, and he and I had grown especially close since I came back from Avoyelles. Even though he and his wife were both in their eighties, Chaplain Rentz was willing to let me come live with them in Baton Rouge. He had even lined up a job for me cutting grass with a local lawn service business.

On the day of the parole board hearing, November 8, 2018, I was ready. My family packed the room, even filling in the empty space where the victim's family would usually sit. It was loud and it was exciting, and for once I didn't have to appear in cuffs and shackles. But even at the last minute, I was still feeling nervous. And a problem had arisen.

The plan for me to live with Chaplain Rentz had been talked about for weeks, and state officials had even visited his house to confirm that the accommodation was suitable. But at some point, at the end of the hearing, someone reminded the board that it wasn't usual for inmates on parole to go straight from prison to living with state officials.

There had been a mad scramble to make alternative arrangements. Help came in the form of the Parole Project, a nonprofit based in Baton Rouge that agreed to take me on for a ten-day reorientation program. After that, Dr. Draper—now Mayor Leslie Draper III—stepped in. He offered me a place to stay, a job working for the town of Simmesport, a role as youth pastor at his church, and even some speaking engagements.

As soon as the parole board hearing began, I could feel myself relax. I knew whose hands my life was in, and I knew there was nothing God couldn't do. I'd been forgiven, so I was free. Whatever happened next—well, that was just up to God.

A lot of the hearing passed me by in a blur, but one moment burned itself into my memory. Mayor Draper stood up to offer his support. He was calm as ever, speaking with the same easy confidence and authority I'd heard on so many occasions at the chapel in Avoyelles.

He told the board all his credentials and described how we met. Then there was a long and uncomfortable pause, as if he couldn't find his next words. Slowly, holding his hand out in my direction, he told them what he thought about me:

"That's one guy I would die for."

48 | RUNNING TOWARD THE EXIT

In the days and weeks after my parole board hearing, I burned through packs of batteries listening to worship music on my JP5 player. One song I had on repeat said exactly what I wanted to hear—that even though the walls around me were yet to fall, I trusted that God was still in control.

Most of the time, when inmates are granted parole, they are taken from the hearing back to their dorm to collect their things with a security officer beside them. Then they are taken to CCR for a night or two until they are released. There's a real danger that an inmate with a grudge might try to attack the parolee, draw them into a fight, or otherwise get them written up so their release is cancelled, so the whole process is well managed and swift.

At least, that's the way it's supposed to happen.

For me, it was different. I was granted parole in the November hearing, but the last-minute change in plan to where I was going to live after my release required more work. The board needed to check things out with Mayor Draper, to make sure everything would be okay for me there.

Of all the time I'd spent in prison, the weeks that followed the parole board hearing were the longest. They moved slower than they did when I was in isolation, slower than the days when I was tempted to lose any hope of ever getting out. I was free, technically, but I'd never felt quite as trapped as I did then.

I did what I could to keep myself busy. I had said all my goodbyes, making sure to spend as much time as possible with Pastor Hicks and others who had made such an impact on me. Eric was in Camp C at this time, and I wanted him to feel encouraged by my leaving, though I knew it wouldn't be easy for him. He had committed his crime as an adult, so *Miller v. Alabama* didn't apply to him. His journey toward parole was long, the view hard to discern.

I gave away the possessions I didn't want to take with me—clothes, shoes, toiletries, and food—and made plans to store all my legal documents and case paperwork in the chapel office until I could collect them sometime in the future. Everything I needed I had packed away in a small black bag. Life had been stripped back to the essentials: a few clothes, some toiletries, a box of letters and photographs, my Bible, and the JP5 player that still reminded me of the timeless truth that fed my soul like oxygen: God had not failed me yet.

Finally, three weeks after the hearing, I was visited by a guard and told I would be released.

"When?"

"Tomorrow."

It seemed to me that I didn't sleep at all that night. I was ready and dressed hours before the exit time I'd been given, my little black bag in my hands.

When the time finally arrived for me to leave, I waited patiently for each gate and doorway to be unlocked. I walked down each corridor, saying a final goodbye to anyone I knew, feeling as if a thousand different storms were all brewing inside me. I breathed deep, trying to keep everything together.

A few more minutes.

Just one more gate.

Soon I'll be out.

Heart pounding, my lungs only filling halfway, I stepped into the final caged walkway. I could see the gate just beyond, hear the car engine running that would take me to the exit. It was all so close. The

end of everything that had happened these last twenty-seven summers. The beginning of everything else.

I took my first step.

What if they've made a mistake?

What if they change their minds?

I didn't know where the thoughts came from, but they weren't
easy to dismiss. So I started running.

The doubts and the fear receded. My arms shot up in celebration.
My hands were waving, even though nobody was there to see me. But
everybody *was* there with me. Everybody who'd helped me along the
way. Mama, Dad, Penny and all my siblings, aunts, uncles, and cousins. I was waving to Tony back in the law library, to Bishop Tannehill,
to Eric. To Chaplain Rentz, Dr. Draper, Pastor Cymbala. To Chaplain
Bernadine St. Cyr, for whom I worked as a clerk for over fifteen years.
To the judge, the victim's mother, to the little boy I'd left fatherless.
To Dawn and her two girls who still called me their daddy, to Teirsen
and the life we hoped to build together one day. I was waving to them
all. I was on my way.

PART 7

A NEW HOME

49 | FIREWORKS AND CELL PHONES

The Mississippi was a carpet of multicolored lights. In the night sky above, great clouds of fireworks were exploding. I was standing in the window of a room overlooking Baton Rouge. I was in awe. All I could do was stare.

"How do you feel?" Teirsen asked. "Are you all right?"

It had been a wild afternoon. At first, when I'd walked through the front gates and saw Teirsen and the people from the Parole Project waiting for me, the only thing I'd been able to do was laugh and cry. I'd then spent a while at the offices of the Parole Project in Baton Rouge, trying to take it all in as they outlined what the next ten days would hold for me. Later, once they'd released me for the weekend, Teirsen and I had gone to eat steak. My phone had rung constantly, with old friends and family all wanting to talk, which set off even more laughing and crying.

But now, for the first time, I could pause and breathe.

I looked around. My little black bag was with me, but already I'd acquired a whole range of new possessions. A phone. A watch. A wallet. All things I'd either had no need for or was not allowed to possess when I woke up that morning. On the counter was a folder with everything I'd been given as I left Angola. Some items, like my birth certificate and my social security card, were things I'd surrendered decades ago. Others, like my certificate of parole and release, were new to me. I was officially allowed out, officially free, yet I was still wearing the same socks I'd put on when I'd dressed in the Main Prison in Ash 3, Bed #22 fourteen hours earlier.

"Ronnie," Teirsen said again. "Are you okay? What are you feeling?"

"I have absolutely no words to answer that," I said. I thought awhile. "Light? Happy? I feel good, but I have no frame of reference for this. I have never felt anything like it."

———

The Parole Project provided a ten-day program designed to reintroduce me to the world. When I'd been arrested, the world was analog; now it was digital. When I ran the streets with Leekie and J-Dog, we had pagers, not cell phones. We paid in cash instead of cards. Shop assistants worked the tills, not closed-circuit TV and self-scan checkouts. And what happened to Walmart? Those stores used to be so small, but when the Parole Project took me shopping in one, it looked more like an airport.

"You can get anything you need in here," I was told as I stared around me, eyes wide and uncomprehending. "What do you want?"

What do I want?

For the second time in as many days, I had no frame of reference for the question. I just couldn't figure it out. But then I saw the part of the store devoted to technology. My eyes lit up.

———

The Parole Project was working with several new parolees like me to help us understand this new world of big-box stores, cell phones, and digital banking. They also put on a series of classes that helped explain some of the other more subtle changes that had taken place in the last three decades. An ex-soldier who had been shot several times talked to us about the challenges of returning home and the importance of good mental health. He likened our experience to his, returning home from battle to a world that followed a different set of rules.

We had a class on how to deal with law enforcement, delivered by a serving officer. I hung on to every word he said, locking away the advice to keep my hands out of my pockets, to stay calm, and to do nothing that might escalate a situation.

But it was the class on sexual harassment that really blew my mind.

I could so easily remember what it was like to walk along Bourbon Street with Leekie, J-Dog, and the others, setting ourselves a challenge about who could flirt the best. We'd go on up and hug girls, tap them on the butt, and say all kinds of things. It was all part of the game.

But now? It stunned me the kind of trouble that behavior could land you in. I could understand that going up and touching a total stranger wasn't okay, but not telling a woman that she looked beautiful in case she took offense, and not telling certain jokes in a workplace in case someone overheard and was upset? It was hard to get my head around how low the threshold for sexual harassment had become. But the Parole Project was run by good people, and they'd helped hundreds of inmates like me make the transition. They listened to my confusion and let me ask all the questions I needed to. And in the end, I figured it wouldn't be too hard to adjust. I'd spent all my time in prison trying to steer clear of female security officers. A lot of guys had enjoyed flirting with them, and some had even gotten serious, like Pastor Norris. But it always seemed to me that life in prison was complicated enough without any of that, so I'd kept my distance and pretty much deleted the part of me that used to win all those flirting competitions back on Bourbon Street.

Throughout the ten-day program I'd been sharing a small room in Baton Rouge with another parolee. It wasn't an ideal sleeping arrangement, but it was only temporary. Besides, it was a penthouse compared to Angola.

As soon as I had completed the program, I said my goodbyes to the Parole Project. The breadth and depth of what they had taught me in those ten days was incredible, and I left there with a driver's license and feeling confident about the challenges ahead. Without them, I would have been a mess.

I headed out to Simmesport, where Mayor Draper welcomed me like I was returning home. He had organized a job and a place for me to live, and I liked the idea of being in a small community of two thousand people. I also liked the living situation Mayor Draper had set up for me: a three-bedroom, two-bathroom, fourteen-hundred-square-foot home with AC, washer, and dryer, all to myself. I spent the first week taking turns sleeping in the bedrooms, picking a different one each night. I felt like I was overseeing my own personal hotel.

There were seventy-five units just like mine on a nine-hundred-acre patch of land on the edge of Simmesport. A wealthy industrialist had put up some money in Katrina's aftermath, and the town had welcomed over two hundred people who had lost everything in the flooding. They were allowed to live rent-free for five years and encouraged to join in the community by learning new skills and using old ones. They called the area Canadaville, and it offered more than emergency shelter. It offered new life.

Almost thirteen years had passed since Katrina, and most of the residents had moved on. This freed up some of the houses, allowing Mayor Draper to do the kind of things he'd been born to do—such as give a parolee like me a home and a job in a nurturing, stable community. I couldn't imagine a more perfect place for me to begin my new life.

50 | "PLEASE OUTGROW US"

I was a newborn all over again, and Mayor Draper was like a father to me. He gave me a job, a town car, and a cell phone for the purpose of work. His church, Tree of Calvary Baptist Church, was the first invitation I had to speak. He got me on my feet, and when I was steady, he encouraged me to take my first steps.

The job was simple enough, but it was a perfect one for me. There was nobody in Simmesport certified to carry out the routine gas checks on each property, and for years the town had either paid fines or high contractor prices. Mayor Draper saw me as a solution, so he sent me away to school for a few days to become certified. Once I was fully trained, I was able to spend my days driving around the quiet rural roads, making house calls, and carrying out my surveys. With so many people to visit, I was in extrovert heaven. And then there was the money. Having spent my years in Angola earning a maximum of twenty cents per hour, the Simmesport hourly wage of seventeen dollars was almost too good to believe. I'd worked almost every day in Angola and barely spent anything over the last few years, but when I'd left, the sum total of my savings was $220. My first week's paycheck when I was in Simmesport—which I needed to be shown what to do with—was almost twice that.

I blew almost all of it in an instant—though it wasn't in Walmart, and I didn't even end up with anything to show for it. I used my wages to pay my $435 electric bill—and needed to be shown how to do that too. It was an expensive lesson that taught me to set the AC to auto—not to leave it running every hour of the day and night.

I was on the receiving end of so much kindness and generosity. Chaplain Rentz and his wife made the drive from Baton Rouge each weekend throughout the first month I was there, each time hauling a trailer full of items I needed. Thanks to them I had three bedroom sets, three kitchen sets, and a desk. Carmen, a volunteer who came to Angola to minister regularly, filled my pantry and refrigerator with food. She also gave me my first little Christmas tree. The people of Simmesport were just as kind. They were patient when I didn't know how to do everyday tasks like using a Weed eater or driving a tractor. I never once felt like I was being viewed with fear or suspicion. They all knew about my past, but nobody seemed troubled by it.

———

I liked living in such a small community, and it felt familiar and safe. One of the many lessons Angola had taught me was the importance of integrity among people. As an inmate pastor, you can't preach about holiness and righteous living and then say, "See y'all next Sunday." You sleep in the same dorm as the people you're preaching to and sit on the toilet right next to them. You can't pretend in there. You have to be honest.

Simmesport was a place where I felt I could be myself. I didn't have to hide my past, and I didn't have to change my personality. I was just me, Ronald Olivier, whether neighbors saw me at work, in church, or sitting on my porch, staring at the sunset with a mile-wide smile across my face.

I liked Simmesport, but I also wanted to go further, to take another step across this new bridge called freedom. Before long I was confident enough to make the two-hour drive to Lafayette to spend weekends with Teirsen and her family. Those were good times too, and I found myself welcomed in by yet another kind and generous community of people.

I felt like I was growing up. Week by week, month by month, I could feel myself gaining confidence. And the more I gained, the more curious I became about this new world in which I had been given a second chance. But when I received an invitation from Pastor Cymbala to preach at Brooklyn Tabernacle, I was excited and somewhat fearful. I'd only been out of prison for several months. Wasn't that too early for me to travel all the way to New York and tell my story in front of thousands of people?

I turned to Mayor Draper for advice, telling him that I didn't know what to think about it all. His response was short and direct.

"Get on the plane! Enjoy the journey. Think about the future when you get back."

It was the answer I wanted but not the one I expected. Mayor Draper had done so much for me already, and I didn't want him to feel like I was not grateful and was looking to get away. "You're sure about this?"

"Ronnie, don't ever feel like you owe me anything. I just want you to succeed. And I know you're just passing through here. Don't get so close that when you leave you break our hearts."

I didn't know what to say. But I didn't need to say anything. I just needed to listen.

"Please outgrow us, Ronnie," he said. "Please."

51 | ONE HUNDRED MILES OF SILENCE WITH WARDEN CAIN

In many ways, speaking at Brooklyn Tabernacle was like nothing I'd ever experienced before. I had no frame of reference for standing in front of so many strangers, telling them about my life. But a part of it all felt familiar too. There I was, running eps about this great God of ours who will stop at nothing to show us how much he loves us.

That first invitation to travel outside of the state and share my story was not the last. Others soon followed. I was invited to speak to the Buffalo Bills in the defense room, at two prisons in Colorado, Cornerstone Church in Connecticut, Christian City Fellowship in Sealy, Texas, and even go on a ten-day trip to Israel. Each time I'd put in a request with my parole officer for permission to leave the state. Most of the time the answer was yes, though leaving the country and flying as far as Israel was never going to happen.

I faced a steep learning curve, but I adjusted quickly and was soon enjoying everything about these trips: the preparation, the events, even the many hours it took me to travel all the way back to Simmesport. Every traffic jam and every delayed flight was just another reminder of the fact that I was free.

Even so, one invitation had me anxious from the moment I accepted it. It was from Warden Cain, and he wanted me to accompany him and another former inmate on a trip to North Carolina to speak at the Prison Seminary Foundation, a nonprofit that Warden Cain—now just plain old Mr. Cain—had founded after retiring from

Angola. He was establishing seminaries across the United States in different prisons and wanted me and the other former inmate, whom I knew well, to share our stories and talk about the benefits of seminary programs in prison.

We could have flown, but Mr. Cain loves to drive, so we set out on a sixteen-hour road trip to North Carolina, sharing the time behind the wheel. I'd spent a lot of time in prayer in the days leading up to the trip, and once we were finally on the road and the conversation dried up a couple of hours in, I went back to praying.

Lord, please give me the right time to address this. You know I've been waiting a long time for this opportunity. Let me know when to talk.

Somewhere around Atlanta, we stopped for food. Then it was Mr. Cain's turn to drive again, and the other guy in the back soon fell asleep. It was time.

"Mr. Cain," I said as we passed a sign that told us Charlotte was 220 miles ahead. "I got something I want to share with you. I've been wanting to share it with you for years."

Mr. Cain kept his eyes on the road. "Oh. Sure."

I took a long breath. "I don't know if you remember this, but years ago you sent me to Camp J for something I didn't do. I was there for eighteen months."

"Is that right?" He sounded like this was all news to him.

"Yeah. It had to do with Pastor Norris having a relationship with a security officer and him having two cell phones in his office. I told you I knew nothing about it, but you thought I was lying. You gave me a polygraph test, which I failed. So you sent me to Camp J."

"Oh, okay. All right."

"I really had nothing to do with it. I'd only just come back to Angola from my missionary journey. And you kept me back there for eighteen months. In those cells. Locked away from everyone and everything."

His phone rang. "Excuse me. I'll take this call."

I watched the road drift by while he spoke. When he hung up, I decided that I'd said enough for now, so I waited. I wanted to give him the chance to come back and say whatever it was he wanted to say. I didn't want to force him, so I kept quiet.

A minute passed. No words. Then ten. Still, Mr. Cain was silent. I sat in silence too. Waiting.

We passed the hour mark, and still neither of us had spoken.

It wasn't until we reached a sign that said Charlotte was now 120 miles ahead that Mr. Cain shifted in his seat and prepared to talk.

"You know, Olivier, I feel bad about that. I know you're a good guy. So, I really feel bad about that."

I had a lot more to say, but I measured my words carefully. "Okay, well, here's the flip side of that story, Mr. Cain. I came to the conclusion when I was in that cell that my life was not in your hands. It was only ever in God's hands. And God gave me another perspective back in Camp J. I started to see it as a mission field, and I shared my faith with everybody who came on that tier. I saw three guys saved and countless others encouraged. And above all else, I got so much closer to God and so much stronger in my faith. So, Mr. Cain, all things work together for good."

This time we drove in silence for a mile at the most before Mr. Cain turned and smiled. "I feel a little better now. Would you forgive me for what I did?"

"Listen," I said, my voice sounding loud in the car. "I forgave you when I was in the cell. If I hadn't forgiven you, I wouldn't be sitting in this vehicle with you. Mr. Cain, all of this is bigger than you. You've been forgiven."

52 | THE PHONE CALL

As soon as I met Teirsen, I knew I wanted to marry her. I told her as much sometime after she introduced me to her sister, Tyra, at the rodeo. Teirsen had given me a look that said, *"Puh-lease!"* But I wasn't deterred. I knew we were going to be married one day, just like she knew I was going to be released from Angola eventually.

Our wedding took place on April 6, 2019, in Simmesport. We had initially planned for a big celebration, but since I had been released only a few months prior and my finances were still low, we changed plans and kept things small. We decided to invest our money in the marriage instead of the wedding. Mayor Draper married us, and we celebrated with friends and family in the fellowship hall at the church, enjoying a night of dancing and cake. The whole day was simple and perfect.

I moved into Teirsen's house in Lafayette but spent the workweek back in Simmesport. Teirsen's two children, Vicki and Jaxon, were fourteen and ten, and I loved being around them, seeing them experience the kind of adolescence I'd never had. I was still able to be in Dawn's girls' lives, too, and life was rich beyond my imagination.

Yet around the time of our first anniversary, I started to have feelings I needed to share with my wife. The world was in the early phases of the COVID pandemic, and like everyone else, Teirsen and I had a lot of time on our hands at home.

"Please don't think I'm not grateful. I am, especially with so many people losing their jobs and all. But the job that I have, I'm getting kind of agitated about it. At times I just feel frustrated being a gas man in Simmesport when I have this great desire inside me to be in full-time ministry. I just know God ain't called me to be a gas man. I know it's part of my journey and I'm passing through, but I'm wondering when it'll be time for me to move on."

Teirsen smiled. "I get it."

That was all I needed from her.

———

Two days later, at about seven in the evening, Teirsen and I were settling down. It had already been one of those days that gave us a lot to talk about. Earlier that day, Teirsen had met with a Realtor who had appraised the house, and we were already in the first stages of trying to figure out where in Lafayette we might move.

My phone rang. It was Burl Cain. He was now Commissioner Cain, in charge of corrections throughout the entire state of Mississippi.

"Hey, Olivier," he said, his voice a little more animated and excited than it had been on the drive out to North Carolina. "What do you think about being head chaplain at Mississippi State Penitentiary?"

I knew exactly what part of me wanted to say. After twenty-seven summers in prison, there was no way I wanted to return, even if I would be on the other side of the bars. It was a world I was more than happy to leave behind.

But another voice inside me was excited by the idea. And this voice was far larger and louder than the one that held me back. Commissioner Cain's offer was coming to me less than forty-eight hours after I'd confessed to Teirsen that I was hoping to move into full-time ministry. Didn't this all sound and feel a lot like God?

"Listen," Commissioner Cain said as I wrestled with the decision. "You get to hire, fire, and pick your team. You get housing and all kinds of benefits. And this is a chance to change that prison in Parchman with the kinds of programs that made such a difference to you in Angola."

"Okay, Commissioner. Let me talk to my wife about it."

"Fine. And when you talk to your wife, tell her I got a job for her too. We need someone to manage the prison's property."

I put the phone down and let the news settle. Let the excitement die down. I breathed deep and prayed hard.

Is this you, God?

I had a hunch that it might be. And I knew for sure that I wanted to do it. But what about Teirsen? Did she really want to move 350 miles away from Lafayette, where not just her whole life but also her kids' lives were based?

Lord, you're going to have to bring us together on this. She says no, we don't go.

———

When I got to talking with Teirsen about the call, I was careful not to load it either way. I just told her what Commissioner Cain had told me, laid out the facts, and let her measure them up.

"Wow." She looked away from me. Eyes wide, staring at the floor.

Teirsen is analytical. She's inquisitive. Before she makes any major decision, she'll do all the research possible, weighing the pros and the cons, the risks and the rewards. And with a decision like this, the cons and the risks were huge. It would mean leaving Lafayette, her family and friends, a job she loved, and the community she belonged to. And that was even *before* figuring out what Vicki and Jaxon might want to do. With Vicki two years away from graduating high school and Jaxon heavily involved in sports with his dad, there was a chance that saying yes to Commissioner Cain's offer would mean saying goodbye to her two children.

I was already doing the math. No way would she say yes.

Teirsen looked up at me. She wore the expression that told me she was done thinking about it. It had taken three minutes, tops.

"Ronnie, you cannot *not* take this job."

53 | CHANGE IS COMING

He was born January 17, 2020, in Lafayette, and we named him Ronald-Reese but called him Ra-Ree. While the world was dealing with lockdown and mask mandates, Teirsen and I were dealing with diapers and embracing the adventures of life with a newborn. I was already a father to Dawn's girls and Teirsen's two children, but there was something special about Ra-Ree. He was my own son, and I'd held him close to my chest from the very first moments of his life. I'd longed for many things when I was in prison—to be free, to be married, to be forgiven—and to be a father of my own child was the final one of those audacious hopes to be fulfilled.

Don't tell me what God can't do.

Ronald-Reese wasn't the only new thing in our lives. We had moved to Parchman, Mississippi, home of the Mississippi State Penitentiary. Teirsen had taken her job as business manager, and I was the director of chaplaincy.

Now, just for one moment, I want you to think about that.

You know it's hard for an ex-convict to get a job. Well, imagine how hard it is for an ex-convict to get a job in a correctional facility. It just doesn't happen. And for me, still being on parole, the chances of working for the Mississippi Department of Corrections were about zero. And yet, there I was, working in the prison and then turning up to meet with my parole officer, parking my Mississippi Department of Corrections car right next to his identical vehicle. It's not just unlikely. It's practically impossible.

Not long before I took the job, the penitentiary at Parchman was in the national news. Riots had been going on for days, fueled by gang violence but made worse by the poor conditions inside. Suicide rates were shockingly high, and murders were common, sometimes as many as three a week. The chances of me enjoying any success were only slightly above the chances of me getting the job in the first place. In other words, I was 100 percent reliant on God.

Commissioner Cain was as good as his word, and I was able to hire and fire as I wished. I brought in other ex-convicts to work alongside me in the chaplaincy department, and together we made sure to spend a lot of time out on the tiers with the men. We wanted the guys to see us, to get to know us, to see that we had no fear, and to hear when we shared our stories. We listened to them gripe about conditions and did what we could to help. We made sure people got the medical treatment they needed and followed up when they returned from their hospital callouts. There was nothing magic about what we did—just a steady flow of respect and kindness.

It didn't take long for the same to flow back toward us. And when a new superintendent came to Parchman—a man with a vision just as bold as Commissioner Cain's—the place was able to really improve. Poor conditions were dealt with, we set up a wide range of programs within the chaplaincy department, and the hold the gangs had on the place was broken. Violence fell by 50 percent within a year of our arrival.

Impossible?

Don't tell me what God can't do.

ACKNOWLEDGMENTS

Thank You, Jesus, Father God, and Holy Spirit, for transforming my life.

Thanks to my loving wife, Teirsen Olivier, whose selfless devotion to our family inspires me to be a loving husband and a great father.

To my kids: Jeanne Bordenave, DeJá Bordenave, Victoria Malvo, Jaxon Malvo, and Ronald-Reese Warren Olivier.

To my parents: Adrian Olivier (mother), Reginald Warren Payne Sr. (father), and Rosetta Payne (stepmother).

I'm grateful for all the family members and friends who motivated and inspired me to finish whatever I started. Space doesn't allow me to list all the names I'd like to include, but you know who you are.

Thank you, Pastor Jim Cymbala, Mayor Leslie Draper III, and Commissioner Burl Cain. Thanks to Andrew Hundley and my colleagues at the Louisiana Parole Project.

Thanks to the Nelson team for making a dream come true: executive editor Janet Talbert (who thought I had a story to tell), associate editor Kathryn Notestine, senior marketing director John Andrade, publicity director Lisa Beech, VP of marketing Chris Sigfrids, VP and publisher Andrew Stoddard, SVP and group publisher Don Jacobson, everyone in sales, and anyone else involved in making this book.

Thanks to my agent, Ann Spangler, and to my writer, Craig Borlase, for telling my story so well.

ABOUT THE AUTHORS

Ronald Olivier served twenty-seven summers in the notorious Louisiana State Penitentiary, known as Angola. He was released in 2018 and became a client of the Louisiana Parole Project. In 2020, less than two years after leaving Angola, Ronald was hired as the director of chaplaincy at the Mississippi State Penitentiary. In 2023 Ronald returned to the Louisiana Parole Project as a client advocate, using his experience to guide other formerly incarcerated people toward successful careers and lives. He lives in Baton Rouge, Louisiana, with his wife and son.

Craig Borlase is a *New York Times* bestselling writer, specializing in crafting dramatic, engaging memoirs. Recent work includes *Counting the Cost* with Jill Duggar and the international bestseller *Finding Gobi*.